FIGHT
FOR YOUR
Marriage

By

ANIKA BARNES CHRISHON

Cover and Layout Design: Chrissi Burrell

Editing: Judith Knutson

Photo Credits: Jin Jae Min, Terrell Petty, and Paul Williamson

I hope you enjoy this book. My goal is to provide practical, Biblical help for restoring unity in your marriage. For more information on other books and resources, please visit: **fightforyourmarriagetoday.com**

ISBN 978-1-7331333-0-2

In Loving Memory of Donita Howell

When my marriage started falling apart, I was under great temptation to lose faith and turn my back on God. However, in His great love and mercy, my Heavenly Father sent His servant, Donita Howell, to befriend me and spark a personal revival in my life. She was in her late 20's when we met at a church-sponsored singles' retreat, but she was wise beyond her years. Donita played an instrumental part in my growth as a Christian and offered tremendous support when I started F.I.G.H.T.ing for my marriage. She not only persuaded me to spend more time praying and studying my Bible, but she also introduced me to important topics like the plan of salvation, victory over sin, Bible prophecy, natural health principles, modest dress, and country living.

I believe the enemy was angry at what was taking place between Donita and me. He attacked Donita's health and her heart. Not only was she diagnosed with lupus, but she also discovered that the young minister who was winning her affections was also winning the affections of a young lady who would eventually become his wife. The news about the young man's unfaithfulness devastated Donita, and her already fragile health began to steadily decline.

Despite these challenges, Donita chose to trust God and walk by faith, instead of sight. In a December 2004 letter, she wrote the following words of faith to me: "God is going to help us and use us to help others, Anika." God helped both of us endure our hardships like good soldiers, and then He saw fit to lay Donita to rest January 26, 2007, at the age of 33-years-old. Before her untimely death, God used Donita to help countless individuals turn their eyes upon Jesus and grow in their Christian experience. It is my prayer that this book will be one of the ways He will use me to help others grow in grace and in the knowledge of our Lord and Saviour Jesus Christ as they lay hold on eternal life and fight the good fight of faith.

TABLE OF CONTENTS

* * * * *

ACKNOWLEDGMENTS

I am eternally grateful to Jesus for His desire and power to save souls and marriages. He heard my prayers on behalf of my husband and our marriage, and He restored our marriage and "the years that the locust hath eaten" (Joel 2:25).

My husband, Brent—The Lord has turned our captivity, given us twice as much as we had before, and blessed our latter end more than our beginning! You were worth the F.I.G.H.T. We've been blessed with a strong marriage and a happy home where we can train our precious children together. I appreciate all of the love and support you have shown me over the last 15 years. Thank you for being my best friend. Thank you also for sacrificing so many of your off days so I could have some extra time to work on this book. I love you!

My daughter, Madison—Thank you for being my right-hand girl and helping me keep all of the boys in line. You are a very special young lady, and I am glad the Lord placed us in each other's lives. Over the years, we have developed a relationship similar to Bible heroines Ruth and Naomi. We don't share the same blood, but the Lord has found a way to bind our hearts together in love. I hope you have grasped the Biblical principles from this book well and never encounter the marital problems your father and I experienced when we were in our early twenties. Thanks also for the extra help you gave me around the house as I worked on this book. I love you, my big girl!

My son, Samuel—Thank you for the love and patience you have shown me over the years. You are growing up to be a fine, young man. Thank you for rolling up your sleeves and helping out with more chores around the house, so I could focus more of my attention on this book. I love you, my big boy!

My sons, Daniel, Anthony-Joseph, and Michael-Shepherd—Thank you for cheerfully letting Daddy take care of you when I had my office time and worked on this book. You are precious gifts from God. I love all three of you!

My mother, Anita McGhee—Thank you for giving me a strong foundation in the Word of God and making sure I was in church on a regular basis. Thank you for sacrificing and working the weekend night shifts, so you could focus on being a full-time mother during the week. Your active role in my childhood has had a great impact upon my life as a mother. Thank you also for continuing to give me a modern-day example of the virtuous woman mentioned in Proverbs 31. I love you!

My stepfather, Ben McGhee—Thank you for taking good care of my mother and for being there for my family on so many occasions. I love you!

My sisters, Anthonita and Abra—Thank you for all the love you have shown me over all these years. I have a lot of fond memories from our childhood days in Woodlawn and later in Tarrant. It means a lot to me that we have been able to maintain good relationships with each other over the years and over the many miles that have separated us from time to time. Thank you for the extra love and support you gave me when I was going through tough times with Brent back in the early 2000s. Thank you also for the interest you have shown in the lives of our children and for showering them with your love and attention. I love both of you!

My stepsisters, Martina, Morgan, and Brittany—Thank you for all of the love and support you have shown me over the years. I am glad we are sisters, and I love all of you!

My mother-in-law, Sherrie Dunn—Thank you for raising Brent to be a strong, independent thinker. The foundation you laid in his childhood has helped pave the way for him to be a godly husband and father. Over the years, he has proven himself to be a strong, loving leader in our home. Thank you for being supportive, involved, and respectful in your dealings with our family. Thank you also for sharing your important and unique perspective when I solicited your feedback for this book. I love you, Nana!

My nephew, Anthony, and niece, Shay—Thank you for letting me practice being a mother with you before I had children of my own. I enjoyed the time we spent together—playing, learning, working, cooking, eating, laughing, talking, and traveling. The Lord blessed us, and we enjoyed many happy times together. We weren't able to spend as much time together after I moved and started having children of my own, but you still have a special place in my heart. I love both of you!

My uncles and aunts, John, Johnnie, Pop, Ava, Daisy, Rochelle, Ruth, Sharon, Shirley, and Yvonne—Thank you for the part you played in helping me to become the woman I am today. I appreciate all of your words of wisdom, your prayers, and the continued love and support you've shown me over the years.

Cousin Kenyatta and Aunt LaTanga—Thank you for the sound marriage advice you gave me when Brent and I were reunited. Your advice has made a tremendous impact upon my life and the life of my family. Kenyatta, thank you for stressing the importance of giving our newly formed family unit time and space to grow and thrive. Thank you also for encouraging us to "leave and cleave" and establish our home in a location that would be conducive to Brent and me becoming united as a couple. Aunt LaTanga, thank you for impressing upon me the importance of not running to my family and friends every time Brent and I experienced some challenges in our marriage.

My former coworkers, Arlethia, Darrell, Deatrice, Edana, Gilda, LaRita, Melonie, Mia, Shonquella, and Wanda—Thank you for being there for me during some of the most challenging and uncertain years of my life. Words cannot express my heartfelt appreciation for all of the support you gave me during the years that Brent and I were separated. Many of you were worried about me when Brent moved, but the Lord turned things around and our love story happily continues. Thank you also for the patience you exhibited towards me on several occasions when I prematurely announced my plans to resign and move to Louisiana to be with Brent. I was sorely disappointed each time Brent and I were not reunited according to my expectations, but I am thankful to the Lord for giving all of us the opportunity to work, cry, play, and pray together for six years.

My friends, Fred and Dawn, Kevin and Tonita, Reggie and Cynthia, Audra, Belinda, Carla C., Carla D., Charmaretta, Clarice, Davonya, Eunice, Frankie, Jamecia, LaQuita, Mark, Paul, Tameka H., Tamika F., Tamora, Tracey, and Valton—Thank you for being my friend and allowing the Lord to use you during some of the most trying times of my life. Your friendship has made an eternal difference in my life and in the lives of my family members.

Chris and Tiffany—Thank you for fighting for your marriage and encouraging others to do the same. Chris, I could hardly believe my ears when you stood up and shared your fresh marriage testimony during the family's Thanksgiving meal at Abra's event center. The Lord used your encouragement for the husbands to fight for their marriages to give me confirmation that I should go forward with my plans to write and publish this book. Tiffany, I really appreciate the timely counsel you shared with me pertaining to the Biblical roles of husbands and wives. The Lord used your words of wisdom to equip me to handle a situation I faced the very day we talked. May the Lord continue to bless your precious family.

Mary—Thank you for encouraging Brent to call me.

Marion—Thank you for coming over and ministering to me the day Brent moved out and for continuing to be there for me as I moved forward and picked up the pieces of my shattered life. I really appreciate the wise, Biblical counsel you shared with me whenever we spent time together. Your godly example inspired me to fervently pray and identify Bible promises. Thank you also for counseling with Brent and me after we were reconciled and for joining us in prayer that God would bless us with a baby boy.

Sheila—Thank you for welcoming the other ladies and me into your home week after week and teaching us how to F.I.G.H.T. for our marriages. Your kindness, hospitality, and self-sacrifice made a huge impact in my life. Thank you for being my sister in Christ, friend, and mentor. I love you, Sheila!

Treva—Thank you for sacrificing your Saturday afternoons and facilitating our health education classes at the church. I learned so much during our year-long training, and I am thankful for the opportunity to share several health principles with my readers in chapter 8.

Dora and Leuanna—Thank you for being there for me, checking on me, encouraging me, praying with me and for me when I was going through some challenging times and feeling low in the beginning of 2018.

FIGHT for Your Marriage **review team, Ann, Antoinette, Aunt Ruth, Dee, Dora, Holly, Isha, Jacquie, Jennifer, Jolayemi, Kadiann, Katrina, Kenesha, Kinya, Lerato, Leuanna, Linda, Merlaine, Myriam, Ntsoaki, Priscilla, Shelly, Tanja, and Yolanda**—Thank you so much for your prayers and for taking the time to read this book's manuscript and offer your honest feedback. Your comments and questions gave me a lot to think about and led to some major revisions. As a result of your feedback, several important details have either been clarified or included in the book. I thought the original manuscript was good, but God used all of you to make it so much better! Your support is a constant reminder that the Lord still has faithful women around the world who are willing to stand for truth and righteousness and F.I.G.H.T. for their marriages. It has been a pleasure collaborating with all of you. THANK YOU, LADIES!

Priscilla—Thank you for encouraging me to share my testimony with the families on the November 2018 True Education All Night Prayer Call. As I prepared for the prayer call, the Lord gave me the idea to use the F.I.G.H.T. acronym to share practical steps that can be used to bring restoration to broken marriages. After I shared my marriage testimony on the call, I felt impressed to move forward with the writing and publication of this book. Thank you for your friendship, continued prayers, and support. They have played a significant role in the development of this book.

Linda—Thank you so much for bringing your God-given talents as a professional writer to this project. As I was writing this book, I struggled at times to clearly express my thoughts. However, time after time the Lord used you to help me choose the right words to effectively get my point across. The Lord used you more than you will ever know, my sister. Thank you for being a part of the team.

Antoinette—Thank you for the great interest you have shown in the success of *FIGHT for Your Marriage*. You were there for me when this book was just an idea, and you continued to be there every step of the way. The Lord used you on numerous occasions to help me stay balanced and keep my priorities in order—Jesus, family, and *then* ministry to others. Thank you for keeping our family and this book in your prayers. Thank you also for helping me prepare the book for publication and for all of the encouraging emails, phone calls, and text messages. I believe the Lord has used this project to further knit our hearts together like sisters. I love you!

FOREWORD

> *And saviours shall come up on mount Zion to judge the mount of Esau;*
> *and the kingdom shall be the Lord's.*
> Obadiah 1:21

I have often thought about the role we may fulfill as actually being saviours in the lives of others. We know we have one Saviour, Jesus Christ our Lord. But, the idea of a follower of Jesus, also being a saviour in my life was a self-evident truth, even before the Lord showed me the verse in Obadiah.

My wife has truly been a saviour in my life, and for this, I am eternally grateful to her, as well as to Jesus. The pages of this book express a genuine love story, a precious testimony of reflecting Jesus' love and salvation. As you read my wife's testimony, you may be perplexed or challenged as you try to wrap your mind around what she did and why. However, think about this: *What exactly is going through someone's mind when they risk their lives and plunge into dangerous waters to save the life of a helpless child who is being swept away to death?*

I am sure the stakes were not apparent to Anika when she prayed for me to return to her and to our marriage union. There was great risk involved in the mission God called Anika to. *What was the risk to her?* Deep down we all know the answer if we think about it. *Why do we not exercise more faith? Why do we not often pray for and expect the seemingly impossible? If we pour our whole soul into an endeavor, how will we carry on if the mission fails?* To give ourselves wholly to pray for and believe in a specific outcome carries the risk of being shattered and spiritually confounded if our prayers are not answered in the way we expected. Therefore, because we too often answer those nagging questions mingled with unbelief, we also too often decline to put ourselves on the line to believe enough to earnestly pray for a specific, amazing outcome.

But what happens if we are plunging into the deep to rescue a soul, and we give only a half-hearted attempt and weaken in the face of cold waves? It's too sad to consider, but that soul is probably lost. So it amazes me that somehow Anika got caught up by God and carried away into a salvational mission for our marriage and my soul! I say she was chosen by God to minister His salvation to one of His children who was lost and drowning in a world of sin. I hope Anika's testimony encourages others to do the same for their spouses who have fallen and departed from the right path.

> *For what knowest thou, O wife, whether thou shalt save thy husband? or*
> *how knowest thou, O man, whether thou shalt save thy wife?*
> *1 Corinthians 7:16*

Thanks be unto God for His unspeakable Gift, Jesus, my Saviour and the greatest Manifestation of Love which the Father of all creation could ever conceive. I am thankful to Jesus for caring enough to purchase and administer an eternal salvation for each of us by the shedding of His blood. I am also thankful for His followers who choose to take up their roles as saviours, working in harmony with the Chief Saviour, to administer His love and Spirit on earth in human flesh.

I am thankful to God for Anika Barnes Chrishon, my wife, who cared enough to pray, believe, and endure that my soul might be saved in Christ. Jesus has provided me with a priceless companion and a wonderful family all wrapped up in the gift of my beautiful, virtuous wife, my earthly savior. Thank you forever.

Brent Oliver Chrishon

PREFACE

arriage is an important institution created by God. After creating the first man, Adam, God said, "It is not good that the man should be alone; I will make him an help meet for him" (Genesis 2:18). God caused a deep sleep to come upon Adam, and He removed one of his ribs. He used the rib to fashion the first woman, Eve. Then, He proceeded to conduct the first ever wedding ceremony and proclaimed the following: "Therefore shall a man leave his father and his mother, and shall cleave unto his wife: and they shall be one flesh" (Genesis 2:24). It is *still* His plan for a man to leave his father and mother, cleave unto his wife, and be one flesh with her. Our Heavenly Father wants husbands and wives to enjoy each other's love and sympathy and be a strong, united front as they train their children for this life and for the life to come in Heaven. With God in the center, husbands and wives can form a "threefold cord that is not quickly broken" (Ecclesiastes 4:12).

However, all around us we see the works of an enemy, Satan. We see "cords" that have been broken and marriages in shambles crumbling under the immense weight of troubled finances, infidelity, and addictions. Satan is a thief that comes to steal, kill, and destroy (John 10:10). He seeks to destroy souls and families. Oftentimes, he attacks the strong heads of our families—the men. "Or else how can one enter into a strong man's house, and spoil his goods, except he first bind the strong man? and then he will spoil his house" (Matthew 12:29). Once he gets the strong man, the rest of the family is often left vulnerable, and the strong man's house can be easily spoiled.

Satan is afraid of the powerful impact for good our husbands can make in our homes and communities, so he prepares tailor-made temptations to deceitfully ensnare them and cause them to fall from their noble, upright positions. Some men fall because they fail to see the importance of keeping a steady job, wisely managing their time and money, helping around the house, or spending time with their families. These poor choices create additional trouble for the rest of the family. Hence, arguments may arise and further disrupt the peace of the home. Other men fall by the flattering words of another woman. Still others fall as a result of their destructive habits or addictions to gambling, pornography, drugs, or alcohol.

> *Two are better than one; because they have a good reward for their labour. For if they fall, the one will lift up his fellow: but woe to him that is alone when he falleth; for he hath not another to help him up.*
> *Ecclesiastes 4:9, 10*

If your spouse has fallen and given in to Satan's temptations, who is the best person to help him up? His wife! Not his mother, his buddy, or his pastor. You are the one who vowed before God to be there for him in troublous times like these. Although your husband was more than likely fairly easy to "have and to hold" in better times, now it is time to "have and to hold" him in worse times—times that may well include overwhelming challenges and surmounting difficulties. Jesus is counting on you to make a fresh commitment to your wedding vows and help your spouse get up from his fall. Could

Jesus possibly want you to exercise care, concern, and compassion for your husband similar to that exhibited by the Good Samaritan towards a complete stranger? Certainly!

> *But a certain Samaritan, as he journeyed, came where he was: and when he saw him, he had compassion on him, and went to him, and bound up his wounds, pouring in oil and wine, and set him on his own beast, and brought him to an inn, and took care of him.*
> *Luke 10:33, 34*

All around us we see the love of many becoming cold, but let it not be the case with us, the children of God. May the Lord instead make us "to increase and abound in love one toward another, and toward all men . . ." (1 Thessalonians 3:12). Helping your husband get up from his fall will serve as a blessing to him, yourself, and your children, if you have them.

It is especially imperative for those of you with children to help your husband recover himself from the snare of the enemy. When husbands are bound by the enemy, naturally-erect protective barriers set up by God are dissolved, and our children become an easy prey for Satan. They are left more vulnerable and are more easily attacked or "spoiled" by the enemy. What are some possible tactics the enemy uses in his attempts to "spoil" our homes and rob our families?

First, when "strong" men are bound by the enemy, marriages often fail. When this happens, mothers who previously stayed at home to take care of their young children may be forced to re-enter the workforce. Out of pure desperation, mothers may go against their maternal instincts and leave their children in less than desirable childcare situations that jeopardize their safety and put them in harm's way. Satan wants to rob our children of their right to grow up in safe environments.

Second, when "strong" men are bound by the enemy, families often separate and a single parent is frequently left to raise the children with little or no support. Countless men and women have done an outstanding job training their children in less than desirable circumstances. However, in some cases the absence of a strong, loving male presence or nurturing, loving female presence in the home may cause boys and girls to crave attention and look for love in the wrong places. Thus, a foundation may be laid for later involvement in same-sex relationships or promiscuous behavior with the opposite sex. Satan wants to rob our children of natural affection.

Finally, when "strong" men are bound by the enemy, divorce is often the result. After a failed marriage, a woman's strong desire for companionship may lead her to use poor judgment as she dates in order to find "Mr. Right." Instead of "Mr. Right" she may go against her better judgment, lower her standards, and settle for "Mr. Wrong." Unfortunately, settling may have a negative impact upon the children. Sadly, many young girls have been violated by their mothers' boyfriends, husbands, or other male friends. Oftentimes, these poor girls are too ashamed or afraid to speak up. At other times, they refrain from telling, because they feel like no one will believe them. Satan wants to rob our children of the innocence associated with childhood and force them to grow up too soon.

We must do our part to frustrate the enemy's plans to rob our families. May the Lord help us rebuild the walls of protection around our family that the enemy has been attempting to break down. "The God of heaven, he will prosper us; therefore we his servants will arise and build" (Nehemiah 2:20). Let us not be afraid, but remember we have the great and terrible Lord on our side as we fight for our sons, our daughters, our husbands, and our homes (Nehemiah 4:14). May we be able to stand like Nehemiah and say, "I had builded the wall, and there was no breach left therein" (Nehemiah 6:1).

The principles contained in this book are indeed contrary to the popular views surrounding us in the 21st century. We are often encouraged to put self first and look upon divorce as a quick and easy solution for broken marriages. However, as Christians we have made a decision to follow Jesus Christ, not the customs of this world. Jesus "humbled Himself and became obedient unto death, even the death of the cross" (Philippians 2:8). Following Jesus requires humility, self-denial, and taking up our cross (Matthew 16:24). It requires following a narrow path of brotherly kindness, love, forgiveness, and reconciliation.

> *And all things are of God, who hath reconciled us to himself by Jesus Christ, and hath given to us the ministry of reconciliation; To wit, that God was in Christ, reconciling the world unto himself, not imputing their trespasses unto them; and hath committed unto us the word of reconciliation.*
> *2 Corinthians 5:18, 19*

Almost 20 years ago, my marriage was broken and in shambles. Through God's amazing providence, I met some women who encouraged me to step out in faith and pray for my husband and our broken marriage. Through a miracle of God, my husband, Brent, and I were reconciled, and now we are happily married.

Ten years ago, I prepared a written testimony and eagerly shared it with others. Although countless individuals looked upon my testimony as a miracle and rejoiced with me as to how the Lord worked things out between Brent and me, most failed to look to the Lord for a miracle in their *own* broken marriages. As a result, I felt compelled to write a book that included not only my marriage testimony, but also practical, Biblical strategies to help other married couples restore unity in Christ.

FIGHT for Your Marriage contains the same strategies I used in my effort to cooperate with Jesus as He worked to bring healing to my broken marriage, but now the strategies are stated in an easy to remember acronym F.I.G.H.T. —

- » **F**ervently Pray.
- » **I**dentify Bible Promises.
- » **G**ive Thanks.
- » **H**ave Patience.
- » **T**ake Time for Testimonies.

I challenge you to forfeit your right to get even or get a divorce. I also challenge you to stop fighting with your spouse and start F.I.G.H.T.ing for your marriage. Regardless as to whether you are surrounded by many, few, or no supporters—this book was written to encourage and equip you as you *FIGHT for Your Marriage!*

PART ONE
ANIKA'S MARRIAGE TESTIMONY

CHAPTER ONE
BOOKS BEFORE BOYS

~-~-~-~-~⟫⟨~-~-~-~-~

"Where's Anika?" "Somewhere reading," was one of the most likely responses during my childhood days in Birmingham, Alabama, in the 1980s. Although I enjoyed riding my bike, watching television, and spending time with my sisters, Anthonita and Abra, reading was nonetheless my favorite pastime. As a result, I looked forward to walking to the library with my mother and sisters, and I eagerly participated when it was time for the library's summer reading clubs. I took my time and perused the countless books on the shelves, and I felt privileged when I left the library with an armload of books. After I read the books, I usually shared what I learned with anybody who would listen.

In middle school, I still enjoyed reading and learning and excelled in most of my classes. I was also well-liked by most of my teachers and many of the students. However, I wore glasses and was a little overweight, so a few classmates who struggled academically and got in trouble with the teachers frequently teased me and called me a "nerd." However, I continued to read and do my best in school. The teasing and name calling eventually ended when I was accepted into a high school for gifted, talented, and creative students where studious behavior was no longer laughed at, but encouraged.

Since I enjoyed learning, I considered becoming a doctor or a dentist when I was in elementary school. However, during my high school years my increasing dislike of seeing blood made both of these careers unrealistic choices for me, so I decided to become a teacher. As a teacher, I could make a difference in the world by nurturing my students and helping them enjoy learning like I enjoyed it. In order to prepare for my career as a teacher, I started babysitting and attending classes for future teachers at a local university. I also worked at an afterschool care program during the school year and at a day camp during the summer.

Around this same time, my maternal grandmother, Grandma Woods, accepted a job as a librarian not too far from my high school. Now I had even more reasons to spend time at the library. During our visits, Grandma Woods and I enjoyed talking, eating, laughing, and working together. I sorted books, answered the phone, and worked at the circulation desk. I also helped her when she led out with programs for children and adults.

Whenever you saw Grandma Woods, she usually had two buttons fastened to her clothes. One said, "**Pray Until Something Happens.**" The other one said, "Those who read succeed." She instilled these and many other important principles in my life as we spent time together. The Lord used these principles to give me a strong foundation. I would need to stand on this foundation when my life started falling apart in my early twenties. Grandma Woods and I maintained a close relationship until she passed away in the spring of 2009.

I was teased so much by the boys in middle school that I was caught off guard when the boys in high school started expressing interest in me. On the other hand, my father knew this day would come, and he was ready. Not only did my father boast of how he would deal with any boy that dared to ask me on a date, but he also started drilling what seemed to be his favorite motto into my head, "Books before boys."

It wasn't too difficult for me to comply with my father's orders, because I was surrounded by other students who were serious about their studies. However, other problems arose. My classmates studied hard, but several of them also partied hard. Monday mornings often brought stories of their weekend alcohol and drug use and promiscuous activity. Although I enjoyed spending time with my classmates on the weekends, the Lord mercifully preserved me and kept me out of a great deal of trouble.

> *Thou art my hiding place;*
> *thou shalt preserve me from trouble. . .*
> *Psalm 32:7*

My "mustard seed sized" faith in God and His Word and my relationship with my parents served as anchors for me during my high-school years. God used the Bible story of Daniel and his three friends to keep me away from alcohol *and drugs*. In like manner, He used the instructive words of my father and the chaste example of my mother to steer me away from *promiscuity*.

I heeded the advice of my parents and focused my attention on my studies. Consequently, I graduated with honors from high school and received a full, four-year scholarship to a university about an hour away from my home. I majored in early-childhood and elementary education and again excelled in my studies. I attended classes and studied during the week, but I usually headed back to Birmingham on the weekends in order to attend worship services and spend time with my family.

During my first year of college, my parents divorced. However, my father didn't want the lives of his beloved daughters to be further disrupted. As a result, he continued to pay the mortgage on our family home, even though he moved out and started renting an apartment near his real estate office. My sisters and I missed having our father at home, but he continued to have an active role in our lives.

The divorce was especially difficult for my mother. However, instead of throwing a pity party for herself, she decided to focus her attention on helping others. She volunteered in the community and planned special events for senior citizens. Instead of complaining about her situation, she decided to count her blessings. Our large home was one of my mother's blessings, and the Lord impressed her to use our home to be a blessing to others.

After church, my mother invited people to join us at our home for lunch. She focused her attention on young adults, singles, and senior citizens who would likely leave church and return to an empty dorm room, apartment, or house. As a result, we often had guests in our home. Often times when guests joined us for lunch, they felt comfortable and in turn invited other guests. Such was the case with Mark.

When Mark moved to the area from Baton Rouge, Louisiana, my mother gave him a warm welcome and an invitation to join us for lunch. Mark was a regular guest in our home, and one bright, spring afternoon in 1998, he brought a handsome, new guy named Brent Chrishon with him. I was leaving the house headed to an afternoon program at church when Mark and Brent arrived. We briefly greeted each other on the sidewalk, but Brent and I enjoyed a more formal introduction later that evening when several of the young people from church met at Mark's apartment.

I was interested in learning more about this young man that showed up at my house. I had many questions. *Who was he? Was he married? Where was he from? What brought him to Birmingham? Would he be here short-term or long-term?* As Brent and I talked, I discovered the answers to my questions. It turned out that Brent was unmarried and had moved to the area from Baton Rouge, Louisiana, for a new sales job. A year prior to our meeting, an acquaintance had shared some life-changing information with him that had led him to do some research at a local library. As a result of his findings at the library, he had begun studying his Bible and eventually had found a church that believed the truths he had discovered during his personal study. Brent met and befriended Jeff, Mark's brother, while attending that church and was baptized at the end of the church's evangelistic meetings. When Jeff heard that Brent would be moving to Birmingham, he asked Mark to look out for him. And that's exactly what Mark did—he looked out for Brent and brought him to my house for lunch the very week he moved to town!

Since Brent was new to the area, I volunteered to help him learn his way around town. My two-year-old nephew, Anthony, often joined us for our adventures around the city. The three of us had great fun as we visited parks, historical landmarks, museums, and other tourist attractions. On other occasions, the two of us, ate at restaurants and attended family gatherings and special events together.

Brent and I enjoyed each other's company and spent a lot of time together. Over time, we became best friends. One morning while we were sitting next to each other in church, Brent looked at me and heard a still small voice say, "This is your wife." Brent liked the words he heard. After he secured permission from my parents, he proposed to me. I gladly accepted, and right away we began planning our wedding. We talked to our pastor about our marriage plans and enrolled in his pre-marital counseling sessions. Then, I focused my attention on our wedding ceremony, our clothes, decorations, and food. I wanted everything to be just right!

Brent and I loved each other and were making plans to get married, but I still remembered my father's counsel to choose books over boys. Therefore, I didn't allow our relationship to interfere with my education. With God's help, I graduated magna cum laude in May 1999, and landed my dream job as a fourth-grade language-arts teacher in the summer of 1999. I thought I was wise and ready for the world, but I was neither one. I still lacked Heavenly wisdom that comes from above (James 3:17).

REVIEW AND REFLECTION QUESTIONS

1. Take a few moments to reflect upon your childhood. How have your childhood experiences shaped your life?

_____

_____

_____

2. What valuable advice did your parents give you as a youth?

_____

_____

_____

3. Briefly tell about a time when God preserved you from trouble.

_____

_____

_____

4. How did you and your spouse meet?

_____

_____

_____

5. Summarize this chapter in one sentence.

_____

_____

_____

CHAPTER TWO

CHOICES

Brent and I exchanged our wedding vows on November 27, 1999, surrounded by a host of family and friends. After our honeymoon in Florida, we got settled in our new home as husband and wife. Brent was learning the ins and outs of a new pharmaceutical-sales job, while I continued to teach fourth grade. When we weren't working, we were usually enjoying each other's company.

Our happy times continued throughout the first nine months of our marriage, but in the summer of 2000 things took a turn for the worse. Brent informed me he was in the process of looking for a new job and making plans to return to Louisiana. His plans to move caught me by surprise, and I was even more surprised when I found out I wasn't invited to join him. We had minor disagreements from time to time, but nothing to a degree that would necessitate separation. Yet, unbeknown to me, Brent was dealing with a lot of different thoughts and temptations. Instead of immediately dismissing the wrong thoughts and bringing them into subjection to the will of God, Brent accepted them and allowed them to guide in his decision-making. Instead of resisting temptation, he yielded to it.

> *Casting down imaginations, and every high thing that exalteth itself against the knowledge of God, and bringing into captivity every thought to the obedience of Christ.*
> *2 Corinthians 10:5*

As a babe in Christ, Brent was an easy prey for Satan. At 25-years-old, Brent found himself in a new city with fairly new, religious beliefs and several, new titles—executive salesman, husband, homeowner, and church-youth leader. Each of these positions of responsibility brought a set of fresh challenges to Brent, and he felt ill-equipped and overwhelmed. Instead of drawing nigh to God and resisting the devil so he would flee, Brent chose to embrace Satan's lies. He felt like everything would be fine if he moved back to Louisiana without me.

All of us have the freedom of choice. We can choose God's way or Satan's way. Unfortunately, Brent chose Satan's way. First, he chose to walk away from God instead of walking *with* God. Then, he chose to live away from me instead of living *with* me. Later, he would choose divorce instead of marriage.

> *There is a way that seemeth right unto a man,*
> *but the end thereof are the ways of death.*
> *Proverbs 16:25*

When Brent decided to leave me, I wondered *How could this happen?* This was not the way things were supposed to work out. When Brent and I were dating, I truly thought I was following the Bible's counsel found in II Corinthians 6:14, "Be ye not unequally yoked together with unbelievers: for what fellowship hath righteousness with unrighteousness? and what communion hath light with darkness?" We were members of the same church, attended church and church sponsored activities on a regular basis, and even held different church offices. I naively thought we were equally yoked. I couldn't understand how such a faithful member of the church would decide to walk away from his Lord, his church, and his wife.

Today I can clearly see what I failed to see as a 23-year-old who lacked wisdom and experience. I incorrectly equated church attendance, membership, and leadership with being a Christian; when in fact, to be a Christian is to be Christlike. It is extremely difficult to be Christlike, if you don't know Christ. It is also difficult to know Christ, if you don't choose to spend time with Him. Instead of choosing to spend time with Christ, Brent and I chose to spend our time with each other, so we didn't really *know* Christ. As a result, we were struggling in our Christian experiences and our marriage was in trouble.

Second Corinthians 3:18 says, "But we all, with open face beholding as in a glass the glory of the Lord, are changed into the same image from glory to glory, even as by the Spirit of the Lord." When we spend time reading the Bible, we are afforded the opportunity to behold the glory of the Lord and meditate upon His goodness. As we allow our minds to dwell upon Christ, the Holy Spirit changes us into His likeness. Bad habits are cut away from our characters, and we become new creatures in Christ.

Therefore if any man be in Christ, he is a new creature: old things are passed away; behold, all things are become new.

2 Corinthians 5:17

Although Brent and I followed along in our Bibles during church services, we failed to regularly study the Bible individually or as a couple in our home. In addition, we failed to constantly inquire, "Is this the way of the Lord?" Our lack of daily Bible study caused us to lack spiritual discernment and vigilance, because we were ignorant of Satan's devices (2 Corinthians 2:11). Consequently, Satan took advantage of our ignorance, and he ensnared us. After we were ensnared, we stumbled, and our marriage failed. We gave Satan an inch in our lives, and he took a mile. He robbed us of almost five years of marital bliss.

Even though neither one of us were exactly thriving in our Christian experience, Brent steadily made choices that caused him to drift farther from the Lord. He headed straight into the enemy's territory—back into the worldly life he lived when he was a university student in New Orleans, Louisiana, in the mid-to-late 1990's. Brent did not strive to overcome, and as a result, he began to misrepresent Christ more and more. Satan ensnared Brent and led him blindly into a life of sin. It would take Brent several years to recover himself out of the snare of the enemy (2 Timothy 2:26).

For man also knoweth not his time: as the fishes that are taken in an evil net, and as the birds that are caught in the snare; so are the sons of men snared in an evil time, when it falleth suddenly upon them.
Ecclesiastes 9:12

I had choices to make, too. I could have yielded to Satan's temptations and gave up on our marriage like Brent or I could F.I.G.H.T. for my marriage. With God's help, I chose to F.I.G.H.T. –

- » **F**ervently Pray.
- » **I**dentify Bible Promises.
- » **G**ive Thanks.
- » **H**ave Patience.
- » **T**ake Time for Testimonies.

REVIEW AND REFLECTION QUESTIONS

1. Does attending the same church make two people equally yoked? Why or why not?

_____

_____

_____

2. What does it mean to be a Christian?

_____

_____

_____

3. How does one become ensnared by Satan?

_____

_____

_____

4. What does it mean to spend time with Jesus?

_____

_____

_____

5. Bible study helps us know God's will, and prayer helps us do God's will. Are you studying your Bible daily? Why or why not? If not, list three ways you can simplify your life, so you can make Bible study a priority in your life.

_____

_____

_____

6. Summarize this chapter in one sentence.

_____

_____

_____

TRY IT!

Make plans to wake up at least 20 minutes earlier each day in order to spend time in prayer and Bible study. Consider beginning your study with the Gospels and dwell upon the life our Lord, Jesus Christ, or use a concordance to help you embark upon a topical study of the Bible.

CHAPTER THREE
A BETTER ALARM

Before Brent and I were married, I would spend the first 30 minutes of each day praying and reading from my Bible and a devotional book. Once we were married, waking up early became increasingly difficult for me. When the alarm clock went off, I repeatedly hit the snooze button. The 30 minutes of quiet time I used to enjoy with Jesus became 20 minutes. The 20 minutes became 10 minutes. Then, the 10 minutes became prayer in the car on my way to work.

My alarm clock was no longer effective in waking me up to spend time with Jesus. As newlyweds, Brent and I spent time together each day, but I no longer made time for Jesus. Slowly, but surely, I left my first love and instead turned my love and attention to Brent.

> *Nevertheless I have somewhat against thee,*
> *because thou hast left thy first love.*
> *Revelation 2:4*

However, things changed quickly when Brent told me about his plans to move to Louisiana—without me. This devastating news was a better alarm—one I could not ignore. I no longer struggled to wake up early as in the past, but I was up bright and early—on my knees, crying and talking to Jesus about my aching heart and confused mind.

When I questioned Brent about his decision to move, he gave me poor excuses. He told me the lies Satan told him. He felt we were married too soon, and he had a lot of things he wanted to do in Louisiana before he got "too old." He shared that his father was a good man, and he had left his wife (Brent's mother), so it was alright for him to do the same. He even went so far as to tell me his mother had survived and that I would survive, too.

Once my mother realized Brent and I were on the verge of separation, she made arrangements for us to attend a marriage retreat. I thought, *Maybe the Lord will use this retreat to convince Brent to stay and work things out.* Hence, I was puzzled and sorely disappointed when Brent refused to participate in most of the scheduled activities. Brent's mind was made up, and he *still* planned to leave. No amount of knowledge obtained from the marriage retreat or counsel from well-meaning family members could convince him to change his mind.

Brent moved back to Louisiana about two months after he announced his plans to me. The day he left, I went to work as usual and had a pretty good day with my fourth-grade students. With the Lord's help, I stayed focused on my job and maintained a positive attitude.

While I was at work, I wondered whether or not Brent was going to go through with his plans. Once I arrived at home, it was clear that Brent had indeed followed through with his plans. His car was gone, and the house was almost empty since he took all of his personal belongings and left me with mine. I was taken aback when I assessed my new reality: No bed! . . . No puppies! . . . No computer! . . . No TV! . . . No alarm clock! . . . No BRENT!

As I looked around the house, feelings of loneliness and sadness overwhelmed me. I started sobbing uncontrollably and cried out to the Lord for help. He heard my cry. He wrapped His loving arms around me, comforted me, and quickly sent help. I don't remember how long I cried, but I remember getting myself together to answer a knock at the door. It was a friend of the family, Marion Henderson. She came by to drop off some items for my mother.

After I shared my disturbing news with Ms. Henderson, she stayed with me for a while and tried her best to comfort me. Before she left, we prayed together and made plans to stay in touch with each other. I believe the Lord sent His servant, Ms. Henderson, to my house in order to speedily answer my prayer for help. She not only helped me the day Brent left, but she continued to help me. I had Biblical counseling sessions (which were essentially Bible studies) with her on a regular basis. The Lord used these sessions to help me cope with Brent's departure and pick up the pieces of my shattered life.

Once my father, a successful real estate broker and owner of an equally successful real estate company, heard about Brent's plans to move, he encouraged me to put our large home up for sale. I took his advice, and the house was scheduled to be shown the day after Brent left. Therefore, my mother and stepfather, Ben, came over after Ms. Henderson left and helped me straighten up the house and get it prepared for the showing. With the help of my Heavenly Father and my earthly father, my home sold within a couple of months! I used the profit I earned to make a down payment on a small condominium and purchase a much needed bedroom suite.

In just a few days, I went from sleeping late in the mornings *with* Brent to waking up early *without* Brent. Now, I eagerly woke up early to pray and to search the Bible for verses to comfort me and inspire me with hope for the future. God's way of waking me up early and getting my attention was much more effective than the alarm clock Brent packed up and carried to Louisiana.

> *I love them that love me;*
> *and those that seek me early shall find me.*
> *Proverbs 8:17*

Jesus says, "As many as I love, I rebuke and chasten: be zealous therefore, and repent" (Revelation 3:19). Out of His great heart filled with love, mercy, and wisdom, my Heavenly Father gently rebuked and chastised me for neglecting to spend time with Him. He also exhorted me to repent. The chastening was not joyous, but grievous. By faith, I believe God's chastening is yielding the peaceable fruit of righteousness (Hebrews 12:11).

My heartache led me to search the scriptures until I rediscovered sweet Jesus, my Friend who has stuck closer to me than a brother. I began to hunger and thirst for more of Jesus and His wonderful words of life. Over time, I developed a deep, lasting love and appreciation for the Bible and its Author. Looking back, I can rejoice and speak the same words as the psalmist, "It is good for me that I have been afflicted; that I might learn thy statutes" (Psalm 119:71).

> *And he shall sit as a refiner and purifier of silver: and he shall purify the*
> *sons of Levi, and purge them as gold and silver, that they may offer unto*
> *the LORD an offering in righteousness.*
> *Malachi 3:3*

As I experienced a revival in my devotional life, I began reading from the book of Psalms each morning before work. As I searched the Scriptures, I found a great deal of comfort and confirmation of the Father's love. My heart was drawn out in love towards Jesus even more as I saw fresh evidence that He understood what I was going through, because He, too, was betrayed by a close companion.

> *For it was not an enemy that reproached me; then I could have borne it: neither was it he that hated me that did magnify himself against me; then I would have hid myself from him: But it was thou, a man mine equal, my guide, and mine acquaintance. We took sweet counsel together, and walked unto the house of God in company.*
> *Psalm 55:11-14*

I started using a Bible concordance to help me find verses that pertained to my particular situation or other topics of interest. For example, I felt forsaken when Brent left. Therefore, I looked up the key word "forsake" to find all the verses that used forsake.

Hence, I was very excited when I discovered the following words in my Bible, "I will never leave thee, nor *forsake* thee" (Hebrews 13:5). I felt as if Jesus was speaking directly to me, and I was overjoyed with His promise to stay with me. Although Brent left me after less than a year of marriage, Jesus promised to NEVER leave me, nor forsake me. As I read passages like the one mentioned, I was convinced and convicted that the Bible was relevant and applicable to modern times and worthy of my time and consideration.

Although my devotional life steadily improved and thus my relationship with Jesus got stronger, my relationship with Brent left a lot to be desired. The next three years of our relationship was like a roller coaster ride—full of ups and downs. There were times when Brent frequently called me and told me how much he loved me, wanted to see me, and wanted to work things out. At other times, I hardly heard from him, and when communication resumed, he told me he didn't love me, didn't want to see me, and didn't want to work things out.

I tried to keep myself busy, so I wouldn't think about Brent. However, this was not a long-term solution, because Satan was fierce in his attacks against me. At times, my heart ached so badly and my desire for Brent's companionship was so strong that I didn't think I could face another day without him. Yet the days, months, and years rolled on. At other times, my thoughts were so consumed with why Brent left and what I could have done differently, I thought I was going to lose my mind. There were even a few incredibly dark times when Satan tried to convince me that life was not worth living anymore, and that I could end my heartache by ending my life. To make matters worse, on a few rare occasions it seemed as if a strong evil presence was hovering over me as I attempted to sleep at night. Thanks be to God, those evil spirits fled when I lifted up my voice and cried out, "Jesus, please help me!"

It is only by the grace of God that I am still here! God carefully watched over me and did not allow the enemy to harm me or convince me to take my own life. God mercifully preserved my sanity and my life. "I shall not die, but live, and declare the works of the LORD" (Psalm 118:17). Hallelujah! Although Satan tried to discourage and destroy me, God overruled and used these experiences to remind me of His unceasing love, watchfulness, and tender care for me.

> *There shall no evil befall thee, neither shall any plague come nigh thy dwelling. For he shall give his angels charge over thee, to keep thee in all thy ways... He shall call upon me, and I will answer him: I will be with him in trouble; I will deliver him, and honour him.*
> *Psalm 91:10, 11, 15*

REVIEW AND REFLECTION QUESTIONS

1. Is Revelation 2:4 addressing you today? Why or why not?

_____

_____

_____

2. What does God do to those He loves? (Revelation 3:19)

_____

_____

_____

3. What does chastening or disciplining yield? (Hebrew 12:11)

_____

_____

_____

4. Think about a time when the Lord chastened or disciplined you. What lessons did you learn?

_____

_____

_____

5. Have you ever been left or forsaken by a loved one? Briefly explain.

_____

_____

_____

6. What promise has God made you? (Hebrews 13:5)

_____

_____

_____

7. Write your favorite verse about God's protection.

_____

_____

_____

8. Summarize this chapter in one sentence.

_____

_____

_____

EXTRA STUDY

Read Mark 14:14-21. Does Jesus understand how it feels to be betrayed? Why or why not?

_____

_____

_____

Day by day, and with each passing moment, Strength I find, to meet my trials here; Trusting in my Father's wise bestowment,I've no cause for worry or for fear. He whose heart is kind beyond all measure Gives unto each day what He deems best—
Lovingly, its part of pain and pleasure, Mingling toil with peace and rest.
~ Carolina Sandell ~

CHAPTER FOUR
MEETINGS AT SHEILA'S

When friends, family members, and church members found out about Brent's decision to leave, most were not shy to offer their opinions. On a few instances, the words were Biblical and encouraging, but often times the words were disappointing and downright discouraging. One couple told me to get on with my life, stop worrying about Brent, and find someone else to marry. Another individual offered to help me "get rid of my problem" by hiring someone to get rid of Brent!

Sadly, most of my church family seemed oblivious to the fact that Brent was no longer around. Brent's absence was like the elephant in the room, and they didn't know what to do or say. As a result, they missed the opportunity to reach out and minister to us—the backslidden and the brokenhearted.

> *Brethren, if a man be overtaken in a fault, ye which are spiritual,*
> *restore such an one in the spirit of meekness;*
> *considering thyself, lest thou also be tempted.*
> *Galatians 6:1*

Despite bleak and dim outward appearances, my Heavenly Father still remembered me. He used His servant, Sheila, to share a glimmer of hope with me. Sheila was the dear woman who told my mother about the marriage retreat Brent and I attended before he moved to Louisiana. I met Sheila at the marriage retreat and briefly shared my situation with her. In response, she invited me to come to her home for a support group for women going through marital challenges similar to mine. My interest was piqued. I looked forward to meeting these women, so I gladly accepted Sheila's invitation.

> *And I will bring the blind by a way that they knew not;*
> *I will lead them in paths that they have not known:*
> *I will make darkness light before them, and crooked things straight.*
> *These things will I do unto them, and not forsake them.*
> *Isaiah 42:16*

I anticipated meeting only Sheila and a couple of other women, so I was rather surprised when I arrived at Sheila's home and found ten or more women there! I didn't realize there were so many women in situations like mine. We were quite a diverse group of women. Our ages, incomes, educational backgrounds, level of Christian maturity, and skin colors varied, just like our marital statuses and family sizes. Some of us attended church on the seventh-day Sabbath while others attended on Sunday. Despite all these differences, we were unified in Christ and by our desire to see Him save our husbands and our marriages.

> *Behold, how good and how pleasant it is for*
> *brethren to dwell together in unity!*
> *Psalm 133:1*

During the meeting we sang, prayed, cried, testified, and studied the Bible together. Sheila and the other leaders shared their inspiring testimonies as to how Jesus frustrated Satan's plans to destroy their families through infidelity, pornography, substance abuse, and other challenges married couples face. None of the leaders said it was easy, but they all said it was worth it. In His own perfect timing, Jesus restored the leaders' marriages and made them better than they were in the beginning.

I believe the Lord was in the midst of our meeting. I also believe He led me to make a commitment to stand for my marriage. As I listened to the testimonies of the leaders, hope revived within me. I started praying and looking to Jesus to bring conviction and conversion to Brent and restore unity between the two of us. I began to believe, if Jesus restored the marriages of the leaders and their husbands, He would also do it for Brent and me.

Needless to say, not everyone was excited about my decision to pray for Brent and our marriage, and some even went so far as to question my sanity. Others were puzzled, yet respectful towards my decision. Take for example, my fellow fourth-grade teachers. They couldn't understand my "odd" choices and emotions. They wondered: *Why is she praying for this man who left her before their first wedding anniversary? Why does she still want to be with him?* Nevertheless, they continued to love and respect me. They were there for me when I needed a shoulder to cry on, a friend to talk to, or someone to cover my class, so I could go cry in private.

Despite the challenges and myriad of human opinions, with God's help I remained committed to the course I had chosen. I started to regularly search the Bible for promises to claim as I prayed for Brent and our marriage. Meanwhile, Brent's commitment to our marriage continued to decline, and he filed for divorce in 2001. Brent didn't have Biblical grounds for divorce, so I refused to sign the papers. Yet, the courts sided with Brent, and the divorce was ultimately granted. Despite the judge's ruling that attempted to "put asunder, what God had joined together" (Matthew 19:6), the Lord spoke to my heart and told me to walk by faith, not by sight. For that reason, I continued to pray for Brent and our marriage.

> *And he answered and said unto them, Have ye not read, that he which made them at the beginning made them male and female, And said, For this cause shall a man leave father and mother, and shall cleave to his wife: and they twain shall be one flesh? Wherefore they are no more twain, but one flesh. What therefore God hath joined together,*
> *let not man put asunder.*
> *Matthew 19:4-6*

Although I was committed to praying for Brent and our marriage, I still needed to learn the importance of trusting in the Lord with all my heart. For the first year or so after Brent left, I read popular books on marriage and watched popular charismatic pastors on television. I tried to follow the advice I discovered, and I even tried my hand at "naming it and claiming it." For example, when Brent left in October of 2000, I fervently prayed for him to return. I went one step further and chose to "name and claim" when I wanted him to return. I prayed that God would bring him back by the end of November, so we could celebrate our one-year anniversary together. Needless to say, we did not celebrate our one-year anniversary together. I proceeded to pray that God would bring Brent back by the end of the year, so we could spend the holidays together. We did not spend the holidays together either.

I must admit I was a rather slow student, but I eventually got the point and refrained from praying that Brent would return home on a specific date. I stopped leaning so much on my own understanding. I chose instead to acknowledge the Lord's wisdom and trust Him to work things out in His own timing.

> *Trust in the LORD with all thine heart;*
> *and lean not unto thine own understanding.*
> *In all thy ways acknowledge him, and he shall direct thy paths.*
> *Be not wise in thine own eyes: fear the LORD, and depart from evil.*
> *Proverbs 3:5-7*

According to 2 Peter 3:9, the Lord is longsuffering and not willing that any should perish, but that all should come to repentance. He loves us, and He wants to save us. However, in His infinite wisdom our Heavenly Father has not instructed us to pinpoint the exact time when a man will repent and return to the Lord. He instructs us instead to pray and not faint—no matter how long it takes.

> *And he spake a parable unto them to this end,*
> *that men ought always to pray, and not to faint.*
> *Luke 18:1*

I wanted Brent to return home quickly because the sooner he returned, the less time I would have to spend answering uncomfortable questions pertaining to his whereabouts. The motives behind my original prayers were rather selfish, but the motives behind my Heavenly Father's answers were always full of love and wisdom. He always has the big picture and our good in mind.

While I was overly concerned about Brent returning to our earthly home by a certain date, Jesus was more concerned with Brent's eternal salvation and making sure he was prepared to receive a Heavenly home. He was more concerned about our spiritual conditions than Brent's physical location. The focus of my prayers changed as my eyes opened, and I started to see Brent and me as sinners in need of a Savior. Our precious Savior was using our failed marriage as a way to get our attention and call us both into a closer relationship with Him.

> *And we know that all things work together for good to them that love God, to them who are the called according to his purpose.*
>
> *Romans 8:28*

REVIEW AND REFLECTION QUESTIONS

1. Is praying for your spouse and your marriage a new concept to you? If so, write five prayer requests on behalf of your spouse or your marriage. Start praying about these requests now. If not, list five answers to prayer that you have recently experienced.

_____

_____

_____

2. I was greatly encouraged by the testimonies of Sheila and the other leaders. Write down an inspiring testimony that made a difference in your life.

_____

_____

_____

3. Think of a time you leaned on your own understanding. Briefly share.

_____

_____

_____

4. Whom does the Lord want to come to repentance? (2 Peter 3:9)

_____

_____

_____

5. Think of a time when the Lord took a seemingly bad situation and worked it out for your good. Briefly share.

_____

_____

_____

6. Summarize this chapter in one sentence.

_____

_____

_____

EXTRA STUDY

1. Read 2 Corinthians 1:3, 4. What has God done for you this week that may comfort or encourage someone else? Write your answer below, and share this testimony with at least one other person today.

_____

_____

_____

2. Read Isaiah 55:8, 9. How do the Lord's thoughts and ways compare to ours?

_____

_____

_____

3. Read 1 John 5:14, 15 and the quote below. List five things we can confidently ask for in prayer.

_____

_____

_____

Christ says, "What things soever ye desire, when ye pray, believe that ye receive them, and ye shall have them." Mark 11:24. He makes it plain that our asking must be according to God's will; we must ask for the things that He has promised, and whatever we receive must be used in doing His will. The conditions met, the promise is unequivocal.

For the pardon of sin, for the Holy Spirit, for a Christlike temper,
for wisdom and strength to do His work, for any gift He has promised,
we may ask; then we are to believe that we receive, and return thanks
to God that we have received.[1]

TRY IT!

List the names of five different families you know. Remember to lift
these families up in prayer when you pray for your family this week.

_____

_____

_____

_____

_____

CHAPTER FIVE
ABRAHAM AND SARAH

M y faith was strong enough to continue praying after the divorce was granted, but it was severely tested in the beginning of 2003 when Brent informed me that he was married *and* a father. This news shook my faith and weakened my commitment to pray for the restoration of our marriage. Yet, when I shared Brent's big news with my close friend, Donita, she immediately turned my attention to the Bible story of Abraham and Sarah.

Abraham and Sarah were an elderly, childless couple mentioned in the Old Testament. God promised Abraham that he would have a son and eventually become the father of many nations. However, Sarah was barren, and there was little outward evidence that this promise would ever be fulfilled.

In the beginning, Abraham had strong faith that the Lord would do what He said He would do. He believed God was going to send him a son. However, as the years passed Sarah remained barren. In time, she became impatient and decided to take matters into her own hands. Sarah foolishly suggested a scheme to hasten the arrival of the promised son, and Abraham cooperated with the plan.

> *And Sarai said unto Abram, Behold now, the LORD hath restrained me from bearing: I pray thee, go in unto my maid; it may be that I may obtain children by her. And Abram hearkened to the voice of Sarai. And Sarai Abram's wife took Hagar her maid the Egyptian, after Abram had dwelt ten years in the land of Canaan, and gave her to her husband Abram to be his wife. And he went in unto Hagar, and she conceived: and when she saw that she had conceived, her mistress was despised in her eyes.*
> *Genesis 16:2-4*

It was never God's will for Abraham (or any other man) to have two wives, as it tears down the sacred circle surrounding the husband and wife and disturbs the peace of the family unit. After being chosen to be Abraham's secondary wife, Hagar gave birth to his firstborn son, Ishmael. Hagar's pride and disrespect toward Sarah caused her a great deal of grief.

In His own perfect timing, God blessed Sarah, and she conceived and gave birth to the child of promise, Isaac. Unfortunately, after the birth of Isaac, Ishmael mocked him. As a result, Sarah urged Abraham to send Hagar and Ishmael away.

> *The Lord, through a holy angel, directed him to grant Sarah's desire; his love for Ishmael or Hagar ought not to stand in the way, for only thus could he restore harmony and happiness to his family. . . Abraham obeyed the angel's word, but it was not without keen suffering. The father's heart was heavy with unspoken grief as he sent away Hagar and his son.*

The instruction given to Abraham touching the sacredness of the marriage relation was to be a lesson for all ages. It declares that the rights and happiness of this relation are to be carefully guarded, even at a great sacrifice. Sarah was the only true wife of Abraham. Her rights as a wife and mother no other person was entitled to share. She reverenced her husband, and in this she is presented in the New Testament as a worthy example. But she was unwilling that Abraham's affections should be given to another, and the Lord did not reprove her for requiring the banishment of her rival. Both Abraham and Sarah distrusted the power of God, and it was this error that led to the marriage with Hagar.[2]

Sarah was Abraham's only true wife. Abraham's secondary wife, Hagar, was eventually sent away. As Donita shared this story with me, she impressed upon me the *significance of Hagar being sent away,* and she even went so far as to suggest the possibility of a "modern-day Hagar" being sent away. I deeply desired to see this "modern-day Hagar" sent away in order to restore happiness and harmony in our marriage, but I had no desire to see Brent separated from his daughter. Things were much more complex now, and I was perplexed. *Was it still possible for the Lord to bring Brent's fairly new relationship to an end? Was it possible for the Lord to send this "modern-day Hagar" away, and yet keep Brent's relationship with his daughter intact?* Part of me continued to believe things could *still* work out between Brent and me, and part of me believed things were clearly over. After three years of fervently praying for our marriage, my faith was slowly dwindling. I continued to pray for Brent's salvation, but I spent a significantly less amount of time praying for the restoration of our marriage.

Not too long after Brent shared his big news with me, I drove a couple of hours north to visit Donita in Huntsville, Alabama. When I arrived, I realized she had company. She introduced me to a male friend of hers, and, strangely enough, my story and his story were very similar. This young man's wife decided she no longer wanted to be married and left him. He and I became friends, and then over time we became a "couple."

As we continued to get to know each other, we began contemplating marriage and eventually shared this with Donita. Much to our surprise, Donita was neither excited about nor supportive of our plans. Instead, she was a bit cautious. Apparently, she had been studying her Bible, and the Holy Spirit convicted her that before we moved forward with our plans to get married, we needed to make sure there was no hope of reconciliation with our former spouses. She went on to remind us that adultery was the only Biblical grounds for divorce.

> It hath been said, Whosoever shall put away his wife, let him give her a writing of divorcement: But I say unto you, That whosoever shall put away his wife, saving for the cause of fornication, causeth her to commit adultery: and whosoever shall marry her that is divorced committeth adultery.
> Matthew 5:31, 32

I was obviously free to remarry, but, if my boyfriend's ex-wife had not entered into another relationship, we could not truly ask God's blessing upon our marriage. Needless to say, I was not excited when Donita shared this with me. However, my boyfriend and I agreed to heed her counsel before moving forward with our marriage plans. In

October 2004, Donita communicated with my boyfriend's ex-wife in order to see if she was involved in another relationship.

> *Hear counsel, and receive instruction,*
> *that thou mayest be wise in thy latter end.*
> *Proverbs 19:20*

As Donita and the young lady talked, she found out she *was not* and *had not* been involved in another relationship. My boyfriend and I were disappointed with Donita's findings, but we decided to bring our relationship to an end. Shortly after the breakup, my ex-boyfriend was reunited with his ex-wife. Meanwhile, I was left alone to pray and ponder my relationship rollercoaster of being single, engaged, married, separated, divorced, single, dating, and single again.

REVIEW AND REFLECTION QUESTIONS

1. Why was Hagar sent away?

_____

_____

2. What are some lessons to be learned from Hagar being sent away? How can you apply these lessons to your situation?

_____

_____

3. How can we keep the sacred family circle unbroken?

_____

_____

4. How can you determine if counsel is wise and should be followed?

_____

_____

_____

5. Have you ever listened to wise counsel that led you to do something very different from what you were planning to do? Was the decision easy or difficult for you? Briefly explain.

_____

_____

_____

6. Summarize this chapter in one sentence.

_____

_____

_____

CHAPTER SIX

GOOD NEWS

In November 2004, a few weeks after my relationship with Donita's friend ended, I received an unexpected phone call from Brent. I say "unexpected," because, for the most part, Brent and I stopped communicating after he told me he was a father in early 2003.

The goodness of God had led Brent to repentance (Romans 2:4), and he was recovering himself from the snare of the enemy (2 Timothy 2:26). God chose to use Brent's daughter, Madison, to begin the transformation in his life that I had been praying for! Madison knew nothing about how Brent was living at the time, but he understood that, as she got older, she *would know*. Eventually, she *would know* what type of man her Daddy was, so Brent wanted to change. He wanted to be a better person. He didn't want Madison to grow up and be with a man like he was at that time. He wanted to change so she would have a better example of the type of man she should be interested in. After several failed attempts to change his bad habits on his own, Brent realized only Jesus could help him change. As a result, Brent began seeking Jesus and a total transformation that only He could provide.

> *And ye shall seek me, and find me,*
> *when ye shall search for me with all your heart.*
> *Jeremiah 29:13*

Of course, as with all of us, there were many other factors involved in Brent's return to Jesus. In addition to using Madison to cause light to break through his life of sin, God gave Brent a disturbing vision about the trouble and thick darkness he was in. Shortly after the vision, Brent's job offered him the opportunity to move from New Orleans, Louisiana, to a much smaller town, Alexandria, Louisiana. Brent desired the move and saw it as a way to make a fresh start spiritually.

Slowly, but surely, Brent began to "grow in grace, and in the knowledge of our Lord and Savior Jesus Christ" (2 Peter 3:18). Eventually, he rededicated his life to Christ and decided to transfer his church membership from the church we used to attend together in Birmingham, Alabama, to the church he was attending in Alexandria, Louisiana. When Brent called and shared his testimony with the church clerk, she suggested he call and let me know he was back in church. Brent's response was, "Anika doesn't want to hear anything from me." However, she insisted, and he finally agreed to give me a call.

As we talked, Brent briefly told me about his conversation with the church clerk. He concluded with the following words, "I am going back to church—not to have one foot in and one foot out, but to have both feet in." I was overjoyed by Brent's good news! This was the moment I had been waiting *and* praying for. Brent was back in his right mind, sitting at the feet of Jesus, *and* on the phone with me! Hallelujah! I responded, "I have been praying for you." Then, he apologized for his past actions and words. It was like a dream, and I could hardly believe my ears! I quickly forgave him, but it would be years before he completely regained my trust.

> *Take heed to yourselves: If thy brother trespass against thee, rebuke him;*
> *and if he repent, forgive him. And if he trespass against thee seven times in*
> *a day, and seven times in a day turn again to thee,*
> *saying, I repent; thou shalt forgive him.*
> *Luke 17:3, 4*
>
> *. . . forgive, and ye shall be forgiven.*
> *Luke 6:37*

As the conversation continued, Brent spoke of his commitment to reestablishing and strengthening his relationship with Jesus. It turns out, as Brent's relationship with Jesus strengthened, his relationship with his "modern-day Hagar" weakened. They eventually drifted apart from each other, and his "modern-day Hagar" left.

> *When the LORD turned again the captivity of Zion, we were like them*
> *that dream. Then was our mouth filled with laughter, and our tongue with*
> *singing: then said they among the heathen, The LORD hath done great*
> *things for them. The LORD hath done great things for us;*
> *whereof we are glad.*
> *Psalm 126:1-3*

The Lord gave me the desires of my heart. His "modern-day Hagar" left, but his precious daughter remained. She continues to be an important part of Brent's life and mine.

After almost four years of praying and walking by faith, the Lord was beginning to answer my prayers in a more observable fashion. From a distance, I could see a prodigal son returning home. It was time to rejoice and be glad because my husband "was dead, and is alive again; and was lost, and is found" (Luke 15:32). It wasn't quite time to kiss him, but it *was* time to have compassion upon him (Luke 15:20).

In the beginning of 2005, Brent and I started talking regularly on the telephone. It didn't take us long to realize we had a lot of catching up to do. We talked about our past and our present, and we made plans for our future. We also prayed and studied our Bibles together.

We were excited about the great things the Lord was going to do for us, and we were looking forward to Him restoring to us the years that the "locust hath eaten" (Joel 2:25). However, as we moved forward, we remembered the past. We didn't want Brent's ungodly course of action to be a stumbling block to others, so Brent confessed his faults and apologized to my family and our church family. They too forgave him and welcomed him back with open arms. After my parents accepted Brent's apology, he requested their permission to re-marry me. They granted their permission. Then, Brent and I started making plans for our new life together.

Typical wedding plans revolve around clothing, food, and drink preparations, and that is exactly how we planned the first time around. I learned the hard way that these types of preparations are not the building blocks for a happy, Christ-centered home. These things have their place, but we should be careful not to allow them to be the all-consuming focus in wedding plans or in our lives in general. Matthew 6:31-33 tells us, "Therefore take no thought, saying,

What shall we eat? or, What shall we drink? or, Wherewithal shall we be clothed? (For after all these things do the Gentiles seek:) for your Heavenly Father knoweth that ye have need of all these things. But seek ye first the kingdom of God, and his righteousness; and all these things shall be added unto you."

The second time around, Brent and I chose a less traditional path for our wedding preparations. We focused our time and energy on spiritual preparation—seeking first the kingdom of God and His righteousness. We laid a stronger foundation for our marriage by choosing to build on the Rock, Jesus Christ, and invest our time in prayer, self-examination, the study of the Bible, and counseling sessions with mature Christian mentors. On August 27, 2005, we re-exchanged our wedding vows in the presence of close family members and friends in my mother and stepfather's living room.

REVIEW AND REFLECTION QUESTIONS

1. What should you do if your spouse commits an offense against you? (Luke 17:3, 4)

_____

_____

_____

2. What must we do if we want God to forgive us? (Luke 6:37)

_____

_____

_____

3. Has the Lord ever turned your captivity? Briefly explain.

_____

_____

_____

4. Summarize this chapter in one sentence.

_____

_____

_____

EXTRA STUDY

1. Read Luke 15:20-24. How did the father in the parable respond to his son when he returned home? What lessons can we learn from his example?

_____

_____

_____

2. Read Matthew 6:15. What happens if we fail to forgive?

_____

_____

_____

3. Read 2 Timothy 2:24-26. How should we deal with one caught in Satan's snare?

_____

_____

_____

TRY IT!

Have you failed to forgive your spouse for offenses he has knowingly or unknowingly committed against you? If so, pray and ask the Lord to help you forgive him. With God's help, you can forgive your husband. You will be blessed as you strive to be a loving, forgiving wife.

CHAPTER SEVEN
MOTHER AND MISSIONARY

~-.~-.~-.~✥❀✥~.~-.~-.~

As our faith increased, so did the size of our family! After our wedding, we packed up my belongings and I *finally* moved to Louisiana to be with Brent. While I was still in the process of unpacking, Brent received an important phone call that would change our lives forever.

His daughter's mother called and asked if Brent's toddler daughter, Madison, could move in with us. Once again, I could hardly believe my ears! With so many negative stereotypes about relationships between stepmothers and stepchildren, I wondered how she felt comfortable entrusting me (someone she had never met) with the care of her little girl. Nevertheless, Brent and I prayed about it and promptly welcomed Madison into our home.

Within a couple of weeks, I went from being *single* to *married* and then on to being a *married mother*. In the beginning, things were a bit awkward between Brent, Madison, and me as we tried to figure out and get adjusted to our new roles and responsibilities. However, with God's help, we eventually settled into our roles and built strong relationships based on mutual love and respect.

While Brent was away at work, Madison and I read books, sang songs, played with toys, cleaned the house, and spent time exploring in the yard. At other times, we hopped in the car and went to the park, the library, the homes of family and friends, or the local church school in order to volunteer.

In His infinite wisdom, the Lord saw fit to place Madison and me in each other's lives. Madison and I needed each other. She needed a mother who would love and instruct her, and I needed a daughter to help me lose self-centered thoughts and gain tenderness and sympathy. Over the years, the Lord has intertwined our hearts with cords of love and blessed us to develop a very special bond similar to that of Bible characters Ruth and Naomi.

> *Although these children are not a part of your flesh and blood, yet through your marriage to their father, they have become yours, to be loved, cherished, instructed, and ministered to by you.*[3]

It was a miracle of the Lord that Brent and I didn't have any children together during our first few years of marriage. It was as if my womb was shut up like Hannah's, the mother of Prophet Samuel. As we made plans to be reconciled in the summer of 2005, I became interested in motherhood, and Hannah's story caught my attention. As I read the first couple of chapters of First Samuel, my heart resonated with Hannah's.

First Samuel 1:10 tells us, "[Hannah] was in bitterness of soul, and prayed unto the LORD, and wept sore." Hannah vowed a vow, and told the LORD if He would look upon her affliction, remember her, and give her a son, she would give the child to the Lord all the days of his life (1 Samuel 1:11). The Lord remembered Hannah and blessed her with a son.

> *Wherefore it came to pass, when the time was come about after Hannah had conceived, that she bare a son, and called his name Samuel, saying, Because I have asked him of the LORD.*
> I Samuel 1:20

After Brent and I were reconciled, Hannah's touching story inspired us to pray for a son. Once again, I began to believe if Jesus did it for someone else, He would do it for Brent and me. Like Hannah, the Lord remembered me. I conceived, had a son in May 2006, and called his name "Samuel," asked of God.

Like Hannah's son, my precious Samuel lived in the "temple" at an early age and served God as a special helper. Brent, Samuel, and I volunteered as missionaries in South Korea for about six months in 2009, and we lived in an efficiency apartment on the third floor of our sponsoring church. However, Madison was unable to join us overseas. She stayed in America with her mother, but we were able to stay in touch with her through letters and phone calls.

Our growing love and appreciation for Jesus and His Holy Word afforded us the opportunity to teach the Bible to Korean children and adults. Brent led out with Bible studies for teens and young adults, while I worked with the children's Bible classes. One of the biggest highlights of our time in Korea came in the summer of 2009 when we organized two successful English Bible camps. Each morning at camp, the children were eagerly greeted by friendly teachers who led out with happy songs, informative health talks, interesting Bible lessons, fun crafts and games centered on the seven days of creation.

At the end of each week-long camp, the parents were invited to join us for the concluding program. They gladly accepted the invitation to watch their children share what they had learned. This was the first time many of the parents had ever entered a Christian church, so we were especially thankful the Holy Spirit led them to join us for these happy moments in the house of the Lord.

> *I was glad when they said unto me,*
> *Let us go into the house of the LORD.*
> *Psalm 122:1*

While we were learning about creation during the camps, the Lord was creating new hearts in some of our friends. At the conclusion of the camps, four young people made decisions to give their hearts to Christ. They were baptized at a nearby river surrounded by their new church family. Brent and I were able to help them get grounded in their faith, and then our time in Korea came to a close. We spent a couple of months in Japan, and then we returned to America in the early winter of 2010.

In August of 2012, I gave birth to our second son, Daniel. Two years later in February of 2014, I gave birth to our third son, Anthony-Joseph. Our fourth son, Michael-Shepherd, was born in October of 2016. To God be the glory! He restored what the enemy took— *sixfold*! The Lord blessed me with a loving husband and five precious children.

> *He maketh the barren woman to keep house,*
> *and to be a joyful mother of children. Praise ye the LORD.*
> *Psalm 113:9*

Brent and I failed to regularly study the Bible individually or as a couple when we were first married in 1999, but things are different now. By God's grace, we regularly study the Bible individually and as a family. Each morning and evening we gather for family worship—a happy time to pray, sing, and study the Bible together. These special times help us build on a firm foundation—Jesus Christ, the Rock. In addition to having family worship in our home, we also regularly attend church as a family and participate in church-sponsored community outreach activities. However, we are careful not to allow church work and activities to interfere with our family obligations or keep us so busy we would be tempted to skip personal devotional time in order to fulfill our responsibilities.

In the early 2000s, my life was centered around my career, luxury vehicle, fine clothes, and large home. Today, instead of getting paid to teach, I teach our children in our home. I no longer drive a luxury vehicle—I drive a minivan. Most of my fine clothes were lost during a move in South Korea. They were replaced by more modest, less expensive clothes that were durable enough to handle life with boys. Finally, instead of an oversized home, we have a comfortable home that meets the needs of our family.

The Lord has been good to our family, and He has blessed us with many temporal blessings. However, instead of placing too much emphasis on the things of this world that fade with the passing of time—jobs, vehicles, clothes and houses—Jesus desires our thoughts and attention to be turned Heavenward. He wants all of us to seek Heavenly things first (Matthew 6:33). He wants us to spend more time thinking about eternal realities and less time thinking about the things of this world.

> *If ye then be risen with Christ, seek those things which are above, where Christ sitteth on the right hand of God. Set your affection on things above, not on things on the earth.*
> *Colossians 3:1, 2*

In contrast, Satan wants us to overvalue earthly things and undervalue Heavenly things. He wants us to get so caught up with our homes, personal belongings, entertainment, jobs, relationships and other activities that we have no time or energy left for devotional time or Heavenly thoughts. This is the path he tried to lead Brent and me on back in 2000. Satan ensnared us and took us captive, but Jesus helped us recover ourselves, and He set us free from Satan's cruel bondage.

> *While we look not at the things which are seen, but at the things which are not seen: for the things which are seen are temporal; but the things which are not seen are eternal.*
> *2 Corinthians 4:18*

We can read about Heaven in Revelation 21 and other places in the Bible, but we can't even imagine the great things God has in store for those of us that love Him! ". . . it is written, Eye hath not seen, nor ear heard, neither have entered into the heart of man, the things which God hath prepared for them that love him" (1 Corinthians 2:9). God loves you. Do you love Him? Why not spend some time studying Revelation 21 to see a small glimpse of what He has in store for you and others who love Him?

Heaven will be full of unspeakable blessings, but we don't have to wait for Heaven to be blessed. "The Lord hath been mindful of us: he will bless us. . ." (Psalm 115:12). He wants to bless our families with unity, love and peace now, so we will be prepared to unite with and dwell peaceably with the family of God in Heaven later. Regardless of how hopeless your situation may seem, your marriage can be restored because all things are possible with God.

My kind, loving Heavenly Father raised me up from brokenness and "barrenness" to marriage, motherhood, and missionary service! Hallelujah! What an amazing testimony of the goodness of God! Now it's your turn. If He did it for me; He will do it for you. Choose faith over sight, and believe that He is working things out for your good. Believe that the Scriptures were written and recorded for your personal encouragement. Believe God meant them for you personally. When you pray, personalize Bible verses, claim them as your own, and believe your prayers will be heard and answered.

The Lord turned the captivity of [Anika] when she prayed for her [husband]; also the LORD gave [Anika] twice as much as [she] had before.
Job 42:10

The Lord blessed the latter end of [Anika] more than [her] beginning.
Job 42:12

When the Lord turned again the captivity of [Brent and me], we were like them that dream. Then was our mouth filled with laughter, and our tongue with singing. . . The LORD hath done great things for us; whereof we are glad.
Psalm 126:1-3

God wants to restore your broken marriage, so get your armor on, and *F.I.G.H.T.* for your marriage!!!

> » **Fervently Pray.**
> » **Identify Bible Promises.**
> » **Give Thanks.**
> » **Have Patience.**
> » **Take Time for Testimonies.**

REVIEW AND REFLECTION QUESTIONS

1. What did Hannah pray for? (1 Samuel 1:11)

_____

_____

_____

2. What should we seek first? (Matthew 6:33)

_____

_____

_____

3. Where should we set our affections? (Colossians 3:2)

_____

_____

_____

4. Fill in the blanks. Satan wants us to _____ earthly things and _____ Heavenly things.

5. Summarize this chapter in one sentence.

_____

_____

_____

EXTRA STUDY

Read Revelation 21. What are your favorite parts about Heaven? Thinking about your answer daily will help you "set your affection on things above" (Colossians 3:2).

_____

_____

_____

TRY IT!

The Scriptures were written for your personal encouragement and edification. Think of three of your favorite Bible promises. Personalize them, and write them below. Refer to these promises often.

_____

_____

_____

_____

_____

_____

My Childhood

My parents, sisters, and me -- early 1980's

My sisters and me playing in the snow

My Sweetheart

Brent and me a few months after we met -- August 1998

My Life as a Teacher

LaRita and me in my classroom -- August 1999

Fourth grade teachers during a bowling fieldtrip

Daddy, my students, and me during a Career Day program in my classroom

My Wedding

Brent and Anika Chrishon -- November 25, 1999

My Family

*Visiting with Grandma
Woods at the library --
March 1995*

*Daddy and His Girls --
December 1997*

Daddy and me -- December 1998

*Brent, Anthony (my nephew),
and me at a church function*

Mama and me -- September 2001

My Life as a Mother

Madison and me at the hospital the day Samuel was born -- May 2006

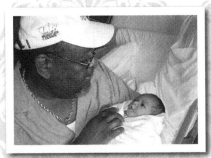

Daddy holding Samuel the day he was born -- May 2006

Family picture taken a few days before Daniel's birth -- July 2012

Visiting with our pastor a few days after Daniel's birth -- August 2012

Baby Anthony-Joseph and Samuel spending time together -- February 2014

Baby Michael meeting his sister and brothers for the first time -- October 2016

My Life as a Missionary

English Bible Camp volunteers, parents and campers–Yang Pyeung, South Korea -- June 2009

Young people who were baptized after English Bible Camp–Dae Hwa, South Korea June 2009

The boys visiting with our mechanic friend in Gangneung, South Korea

Samuel and Daniel at Gilead Valley Health Retreat, South Korea

Our last Sabbath with our church family in Gangneung, South Korea -- October 2015

Spending time with our Korean friends shortly before we returned to America – October 2015

Front row: Daniel, Han Byeol, Samuel, Tae Hyun
Back row: Hye Won, Anika, Anthony, Brent and Yae Lim

My Family Today

All seven of us at the church where Brent and I were married with the pastor who married us twenty years ago -- April 2019

PART TWO

HOW TO F.I.G.H.T.
FOR YOUR MARRIAGE

CHAPTER EIGHT
G.E.T. R.E.A.D.Y. to F.I.G.H.T.

1. Identify the Real Enemy

When Brent left I was confused and had many questions. *How did this happen? What could I have done differently? Where do I go from here? Should I wait for Brent or move on?*

> *In thee, O LORD, do I put my trust: let me never be put to confusion.*
> *Psalm 71:1*

My loving Heavenly Father used the first meeting at Sheila's home to bring me a great deal of clarity and hope. I am so thankful for the love and support Sheila and the other ladies gave me during that very difficult time of my life. They reassured me of God's love and His plans for me, lifted me up in prayer, consoled me when I cried, and showered me with encouraging phone calls and cards at just the right times. Since they had walked (or in some cases were walking) the road I was traveling, they were able to minister to my needs. These sisters helped me take my eyes off the one who left me and turn my eyes upon Jesus, the One who promised He would never leave me nor forsake me (Hebrews 13:5).

> *Who comforteth us in all our tribulation, that we may be able to comfort*
> *them which are in any trouble, by the comfort wherewith*
> *we ourselves are comforted of God.*
> *2 Corinthians 1:4*

I cannot personally meet each reader of this book and duplicate the love and support I received from the godly women that regularly met at Sheila's home, but I can share encouraging Bible verses to remind you of our Heavenly Father's great love and of His desire to heal you and your marriage. He loves you with an everlasting love and has drawn you with lovingkindness (Jeremiah 31:3). He is close to those with broken hearts (Psalm 34:18). He also heals the broken in heart and binds up their wounds (Psalm 147:3). I can also share indispensable "weapons" that will assist you in your F.I.G.H.T. for your marriage.

> *For the weapons of our warfare are not carnal, but mighty through God to*
> *the pulling down of strongholds; Casting down imaginations, and every*
> *high thing that exalteth itself against the knowledge of God, and bringing*
> *into captivity every thought to the obedience of Christ.*
> *2 Corinthians 10:4, 5*

We are Christian soldiers, and Jesus is our General. In order to accomplish our mission and win the F.I.G.H.T., we must faithfully do our part, yet rely upon and stay connected with Jesus for success. This connection is formed when we lift up our voices in prayer and become accustomed to hearing His voice as He speaks to us through the promptings of His Holy Spirit and through the writings of the Bible, the Christian soldier's handbook. We must read and obey

His orders as outlined in the Bible and use only the weapons He provides for us. After we've done our part, we can trust Jesus to gain the victory for us, because the battle is not ours, but His (2 Chronicles 20:15).

Before you begin to F.I.G.H.T., you must identify the correct enemy or adversary. Your spouse is not the enemy (Ephesians 6:12). The real enemy is Satan or the devil and his host of evil angels. Satan is a thief, and he wants to steal peace and happiness from your home (John 10:10).

> *Be sober, be vigilant; because your adversary the devil, as a roaring lion, walketh about, seeking whom he may devour.*
> *I Peter 5:8*

Satan has targeted and attacked families from the very beginning of time and is still attacking families. He tempted the first woman, Eve, who committed the first human sin by eating forbidden fruit from the tree of knowledge of good and evil (Genesis 3:6). Eve's firstborn son, Cain, later committed the world's first murder after he became angry with his brother, Abel. Genesis 4:8 states, "And Cain talked with Abel his brother: and it came to pass, when they were in the field, that Cain rose up against Abel his brother, and slew him." As a result of Eve's poor choice, the histories of earth's families have been filled with sadness, sickness, and sin. This is not God's ideal for families. He wants husbands, wives, and children to be happy, healthy, and holy.

Satan's reign of terror as the prince of this world has continued for 6,000 years, but it will come to an end at Jesus' second coming. At that time, the kingdoms of this world will become the kingdoms of our Lord, and He shall reign forever and ever (Revelation 11:15). Let us watch and pray, so we will be prepared to join Him in His perfect, peaceful kingdom.

Now that you have identified the real enemy, Satan, it is time to put your armor on.

2. Put on the Whole Armor of God

Wherefore take unto you the whole armour of God, that ye may be able to withstand in the evil day, and having done all, to stand. Stand therefore, having your loins girt about with truth, and having on the breastplate of righteousness; And your feet shod with the preparation of the gospel of peace; Above all, taking the shield of faith, wherewith ye shall be able to quench all the fiery darts of the wicked. And take the helmet of salvation, and the sword of the Spirit, which is the word of God: Praying always with all prayer and supplication in the Spirit, and watching thereunto with all perseverance and supplication for all saints.

Ephesians 6:13-18

The weapons Paul mentions above are literal pieces of armor used in actual real-time battles, but they also have spiritual applications that can help Christian soldiers F.I.G.H.T. Shortly after Brent chose to walk away from God and our marriage in 2000, the Lord led me to the meetings at Sheila's and prompted me to F.I.G.H.T. for my marriage. I had a desire to see my marriage restored, but I was a babe in Christ and lacked the armor of God. As a result, F.I.G.H.T.ing for my marriage was extremely difficult for me in the beginning. Instead of having my loins girded with truth, I listened to the enemy's lies and focused on my weaknesses and inabilities—not God's strength and His abilities. At the same time, I lacked the ability to skillfully use the sword of the Spirit, God's Word. I spent so much time watching television I had very little time left for prayer and Bible study. Thus, I was very familiar with the ways and words of my favorite actors and actresses, but significantly less familiar with the ways and words of God. Since I failed to use my time wisely, I was spiritually weak and lacked the strength I needed to consistently lift up the shield of faith and quench the enemy's fiery darts.

In the midst of my failings and shortcomings, once again my merciful Heavenly Father remembered me and sent help. One afternoon while visiting in the home of some family members, I noticed a Bible verse posted on a bathroom door. It said, "Finally, brethren, whatsoever things are true, whatsoever things are honest, whatsoever things are just, whatsoever things are pure, whatsoever things are lovely, whatsoever things are of good report; if there be any virtue, and if there be any praise, think on these things" (Philippians 4:8). The Lord eventually used this verse to change my thoughts and the way I spent my time.

Throughout my childhood and into my early twenties, watching television was a huge part of my life. As a child, I hurriedly finished my homework so I could kick back and enjoy the latest cartoons, music videos and sitcoms. When I began my career as a teacher, I often watched television from the time I got home from work until I went to bed. However, things started changing after I became familiar with the principles mentioned in Philippians 4:8. I started watching my favorite television shows with fresh eyes, and I quickly realized most were not true, honest, just, pure, lovely, or virtuous. I continued to turn on the television after work, but in a short amount of time I went from watching three to four hours of television each evening to hardly any television at all. Eventually, I was convicted that even the "good, clean" shows were suggestive in nature and subtly promoting immoral activities. Thus, I got rid of my television. Consequently, I went from having "no time" to read my Bible to having plenty of time to pray, study my Bible and develop a closer relationship with Jesus.

With God's help, I slowly began putting my armor on. First, He taught me to gird my loins with truth. I was no longer filling my mind with untrue stories created in Hollywood, but I was studying the Bible and storing its precious truths in my mind. As I continued to study my Bible, I became more skillful in using the sword of the Spirit as a defense against the lies of the enemy. When the enemy came to me with his lies, the Holy Spirit brought fitting truths from the Bible to my remembrance and encouraged me to walk by faith, not by sight. As I spent more time praying and studying my Bible, my faith strengthened, and I was able to lift the shield of faith and quench the fiery darts of the enemy. As time passed, I continued to put my armor on until I was equipped and prepared to F.I.G.H.T. for my marriage.

God gives us weapons that are not carnal, but mighty to pull down strongholds (2 Corinthians 10:4). Paul, the author of 2 Corinthians, could speak so confidently about these weapons because he was given the opportunity to be a firsthand witness to the power of these weapons. Paul watched these mighty weapons pull down strongholds during his imprisonment in Rome during the reign of Nero, a ruler who was known for his hatred of Christians. The character of Nero's attendants and courtiers were very similar to his—fierce, debased and corrupt. This atmosphere was extremely uncongenial to the spread of Christianity, yet God's mighty weapons were able to pull down strongholds in Nero's household and converts to Christianity were made (Philippians 4:22).

God's weapons were also powerful enough to pull down the strongholds of infidelity, pornography, and substance abuse in the marriages of the praying wives that met at Sheila's house. These mighty weapons pulled down the strongholds that were binding Brent, too. Today, they can be used to pull down whatever strongholds you may be facing in your marriage.

As a prisoner in the midst of a long, unjust imprisonment in Rome, Paul's patience, cheerfulness, courage, and faith were like a continual sermon to those around him. How about you? Could your patience, cheerfulness, courage, and faith in the midst of a broken marriage serve as a continual sermon to your spouse? Certainly! The following Bible passage reveals the blessings that may result when we choose to be Christlike in our homes—even when the conditions are less than desirable:

> *Likewise, ye wives, be in subjection to your own husbands; that, if any obey not the word, they also may without the word be won by the conversation of the wives; While they behold your chaste conversation coupled with fear. Whose adorning let it not be that outward adorning of plaiting the hair, and of wearing of gold, or of putting on of apparel; But let it be the hidden man of the heart, in that which is not corruptible, even the ornament of a meek and quiet spirit, which is in the sight of God of great price.*
> *1 Peter 3:1-4*

If we choose to be Christlike in our homes, our spouses may be won to the cause of Christ. Hallelujah! No wonder Jesus tells us in Matthew 11:28, 29 that we shall find rest unto our souls when we learn of Him and of His meekness and lowliness of heart. His ways are certainly higher than our ways. May He help all of us come up higher and find rest unto our souls.

May your spouse one day be able to proclaim like David, ". . .thy gentleness hath made me great!" (2 Samuel 22:36). I hope you are getting the point. With God's help, refrain from using Satan's readily available weapons. Put away the bad attitude, the refusals to talk, the rolling eyes and necks, the hands on the hips, and any other non-Heaven approved tactics you have used in the past. Choose Christ's methods instead. Follow the example of meek and lowly Jesus—hold your peace (Matthew 26:63) and let the law of kindness be upon your lips (Proverbs 31:26). Remember, "A soft answer turneth away wrath: but grievous words stir up anger (Proverbs 15:1).

Yes, our husbands may do things that offend us, but two wrongs don't make a right. Catching an attitude may seem like an effective way of dealing with our spouses, but we can't use Satan's methods and expect to get good, lasting results in the end. Satan's methods may appear to help us win a battle, but we want to win the entire war—not just a battle here or there. Keep the big picture and the end in mind. Our ultimate goal is to see our husbands saved and growing in grace and in the knowledge of our Lord and Savior Jesus. Therefore, it would be well for us to consider the following quote as we deal with our spouses and others:

> *Christ's method alone will give true success in reaching the people. The Saviour mingled with men as one who desired their good. He showed His sympathy for them, ministered to their needs, and won their confidence. Then He bade them, "Follow Me."*[4]

May the Holy Spirit come into our hearts, make us new creatures, and help us choose Christ's methods in our dealings with our husbands and others (2 Corinthians 5:17).

3. G.E.T. R.E.A.D.Y.

> *And every man that striveth for the mastery is temperate in all things.*
> *Now they do it to obtain a corruptible crown; but we an incorruptible.*
> *1 Corinthians 9:25*

Before they are ordered to the battlefield, soldiers typically go through comprehensive basic training. This training helps the soldiers to be physically and mentally prepared for battle at a moment's notice. Similarly, Christian soldiers must undergo extensive training in order to be physically, mentally, and spiritually prepared to "stand against the wiles of the devil" (Ephesians 6:11).

There are eight health principles that will greatly assist you as you F.I.G.H.T. for your marriage. G.E.T. R.E.A.D.Y. is an acronym that can help you remember these important life changing, life-sustaining principles that will positively impact your physical, mental, and spiritual health. More specifically, incorporating these principles can have a soothing effect upon your nerves and help you have a clear, sound mind that is receptive to the promptings of the Holy Spirit and ready to obey Heavenly orders.

» **G**et fresh air daily.
» **E**xercise regularly.
» **T**rust in God.

» **R**etire for the night by 10:00 PM.

» **E**at healthy foods.

» **A**im to get 15 minutes of sunlight daily.

» **D**rink lots of water.

» **Y**ield not to drugs and alcohol.

*Please see the appendix for more details about these eight health principles.

Now that you have identified the real enemy and become more acquainted with the weapons of Christian soldiers and the eight health principles, you are ready to advance and take a closer look at the five practical, Biblical principles that form the basis of the F.I.G.H.T. acronym.

» **F**ervently Pray.

» **I**dentify Bible Promises.

» **G**ive Thanks.

» **H**ave Patience.

» **T**ake Time for Testimonies.

REVIEW AND REFLECTION QUESTIONS

1. Read 1 Peter 3:1-4. Use a Bible concordance or dictionary to look up the following words. Write the definitions below.

Chaste:

_____

_____

Meek:

_____

_____

What is more important in the sight of God, your clothes or your character? Why?

_____

_____

_____

2. Would you describe yourself as meek, lowly, and quiet? Why or why not?

_____

_____

_____

3. Would your spouse describe you as meek, lowly, and quiet? Why or why not?

_____

_____

_____

4. Are you using heaven-approved tactics in your dealings with your spouse? If not, list the areas that need improvement. Be sure to include these areas in your prayers.

_____

_____

_____

5. Write out the eight health principles that will prepare you to be physically, mentally, and spiritually prepared to "stand against the wiles of the devil" and F.I.G.H.T. for your marriage.

G _____

E _____

T _____

R _____

E _____

A _____

D _____

Y _____

Which of these eight areas are you the strongest in? (Keep up the good work!)

_____

_____

Which of these eight areas are you the weakest in?

_____

_____

Make a realistic goal and start improving in your weakest area this week. (You can do it!)

MY GOAL:

_____

_____

_____

6. Summarize this chapter in one sentence.

_____

_____

EXTRA STUDY

1. Read Proverbs 20:1. Is it wise to drink wine?

_____

_____

2. Read Proverbs 23:29-35. What are some of the troubles associated with wine drinking?

_____

_____

3. Read Galatians 5:22, 23. List the character qualities that will be manifested in our lives when the Holy Spirit dwells in our hearts.

_____

_____

TRY IT!

Impatience and irritability are a couple of the symptoms associated with dehydration. The next time you feel like giving someone a "piece of your mind," grab a glass of water and pray instead.

FURTHER STUDY:

- » *Healthy Self:* 10 Habits of the Longest Living Americans by Rico Hill and Jared Thurmon. This book will take you on a 10-week journey designed to educate, equip, and empower you to take responsibility for your health through simple, inexpensive, and natural lifestyle practices.

- » *Natural Remedies Encyclopedia* by Vance Ferrell and Harold M. Cherne, M.D. This book offers 11,000 inexpensive home remedies and covers over 730 diseases and disorders.

- » *7 Secrets Cookbook* by Neva & Jim Brackett. The authors of this book share seven simple skills and numerous recipes that will help you prepare healthy, delicious plant-based meals.

- » *Sunlight* by Dr. Zane Kime. This book contains scientific information pertaining to the benefits of sunlight and how to enjoy sunlight safely.

- » If you would like to learn more about the 8 laws of health from a medical professional, please contact me. My email address is: anika@fightforyourmarriagetoday.com

It's time to put your armor on, and F.I.G.H.T. for your marriage!

CHAPTER NINE

FERVENTLY PRAY

> *The effectual fervent prayer of a righteous man availeth much.*
> *James 5:16*

I must confess—I cried more than I prayed the day Brent left me. The tears started flowing the evening I returned home from work and saw empty spaces that were once filled with Brent's belongings. The tears continued to flow as I realized Brent was *really* gone. I probably would have spent the entire evening crying, if my mother's friend, my mother, and my stepfather had not come to my home.

Sometimes soldiers cry. Jesus cried over the doomed and beloved city of Jerusalem (Luke 19:41). David, the fearless soldier who killed giant Goliath, cried so much he watered his couch with his tears (Psalm 6:6). In another place David says, "I am weary of my crying: my throat is dried" (Psalm 69:3). Paul, who courageously admonishes us to put on the whole armour of God, says he served the Lord with all humility of mind, and with many tears (Acts 20:19). If you have shed tears over your spouse, your marriage, or anything else, you are not alone—other soldiers have cried.

> *We are soldiers in the army.*
> *We have to fight although we have to cry.*
> *We've got to hold up the blood-stained banner.*
> *We've got to hold it up until we die!*
> *~Author Unknown*

There are times when soldiers cry, and there are times when soldiers must endure hardness, fervently pray, and persevere. Although I felt like crying until Brent changed his mind and returned home, I had to bring my crying to an end. I could not put my life on hold because of my marriage troubles. I had commitments to keep, responsibilities to fulfill, and bills to pay, so with God's help, I went to work and faced my co-workers and students the next day.

As a result of sin entering our world, trials and affliction are a part of life. "Many are the afflictions of the righteous: but the LORD delivereth him out of them all" (Psalm 34:19). Paul and Silas were godly soldiers who were familiar with trials and affliction. On one occasion they were accused of troubling the city of Philippi, because they were preaching the Gospel of deliverance. The city rulers beat and threw them into prison. What did these two faithful soldiers do while in prison? Acts 16:25 tells us in the midst of trials and afflictions, these soldiers chose to pray and sing praises to God. What an example for us to follow!

"Is any among you afflicted? Let him pray "(James 5:13). This is exactly what Paul and Silas did in the midst of their affliction, and this is what we need to do in the midst of ours. Did God hear their prayers? Yes! Did God deliver them from their affliction? He certainly did! Acts 16:26 states, "And suddenly there was a great earthquake, so that the foundations of the prison were shaken: and immediately all the doors were opened, and every one's bands were loosed." Paul and Silas fervently prayed, and God showed Himself to be a Mighty Deliverer. When we fervently pray, God is willing and able to do the same for us. The eyes of the LORD run to and fro throughout the whole earth, to show himself strong in the behalf of them whose heart is perfect toward him (2 Chronicles 16:9). How encouraging! God wants to show Himself strong on our behalf.

After Brent left, I realized my brief morning prayers were inadequate. Gone were the days of five to ten minutes of praying or failing to pray at all. I was much too needy to spend so little time in prayer. I felt unloved and forsaken, and I *needed* Jesus to reassure me of His love and His commitment to never leave me nor forsake me. I also needed Jesus to comfort me, give me a personal revival, and heal my broken heart and broken marriage. Jesus and I had a lot of catching up to do, so as time passed, thirty minutes of prayer was hardly enough time.

As I spent more time in prayer, I was rewarded with much needed strength. The Lord transformed me from a timid babe in Christ stretched out prostrate on the floor with lots of weeping and little prayer to an armed soldier ready to boldly approach the throne of grace in order to obtain mercy and help in my great time of need (Hebrews 4:16). As my prayers for comfort, healing, and personal revival were answered, my faith increased. Pretty soon, I had enough faith to believe the Lord would heal my broken marriage like He was healing my broken heart.

When souls and marriages are on the line, fervent prayer is a necessity. Faith and perseverance are two important elements of fervent prayer. Hebrews 11:6 states, "But without faith it is impossible to please him: for he that cometh to God must believe that he is, and that he is a rewarder of them that diligently seek him." The importance of praying in faith is also expressed in Matthew 21:22, "And all things, whatsoever ye shall ask in prayer, believing, ye shall receive." When we go to God in prayer, we must ask according to His will and have faith that He will hear and answer our prayers. Then we must patiently wait and have confidence that He will give us anything we ask according to His will (I John 5:14, 15).

We can trust God and pray in faith because the Lord God is abundant in goodness and truth (Exodus 34:6). Just and true are His ways (Revelation 15:3). Furthermore, God is not a man, that he should lie; neither the son of man, that he should repent: hath he said, and shall he not do it? or hath he spoken, and shall he not make it good? (Numbers 23:19). If God says He is going to do something, we can have confidence that He will do what He says He will do.

If results are not immediate, persevere in prayer. Be not weary in well doing. Earnestly and sincerely wrestle like Jacob in prayer, and don't let go until God blesses you. No matter what you see, how you feel, or how long it takes—keep praying!

Fervent prayer is an indispensable weapon—for it connects us to the throne of our Heavenly Father. He delights to hear and provide deliverance in response to the effectual, fervent prayers of His children. As parents typically enjoy giving gifts to their children, our Heavenly Father finds even greater joy in giving good things to His children who ask. In Matthew 7:7, 8, He follows up an illustration about fervent prayer with the words: "Ask, and it shall be given you; seek, and ye shall find; knock, and it shall be opened unto you: For every one that asketh receiveth; and he that seeketh findeth; and to him that knocketh it shall be opened." If we ask in faith, God promises to answer.

Soldier, make a decision to fervently pray and have faith in God's Word—it shall not return unto Him void, but it will accomplish that which He pleases, and it will prosper where He sends it (Isaiah 55:11). Let's go forward, and *Identify Bible Promises* that will enhance your fervent prayers.

REVIEW AND REFLECTION QUESTIONS

1. What kind of prayer produces results? Describe this type of prayer. (James 5:16)

_____

_____

_____

2. What should we do when we are afflicted? (James 5:13)

_____

_____

_____

3. What does God want to do for you? (2 Chronicles 16:9, first part)

_____

_____

_____

4. List areas in your life where you need God to show Himself strong on your behalf. Fervently pray for each item on your list daily.

_____

_____

_____

5. What are two important elements of fervent prayer?

_____

_____

_____

6. Summarize this chapter in one sentence.

_____

_____

_____

EXTRA STUDY

1. Read Psalm 55:17 and Daniel 6:10. How many times a day did these Christian soldiers pray?

_____

_____

_____

As you take time to eat and care for your physical needs, be sure to set aside time to pray and take care of your spiritual needs.

2. Jesus is our perfect Example. Read Mark 1:35, Luke 5:16, 6:12 and 22:41, 44. Describe Jesus' manner of prayer.

_____

_____

_____

3. Read Exodus 34:6, 7. What are some words used to describe God's character? How does this description help you have faith in God?

_____

_____

_____

4. Read Luke 11:5-10. What can we learn about prayer from this illustration?

_____

_____

_____

CHAPTER TEN

IDENTIFY BIBLE PROMISES

> *Whereby are given unto us exceeding great and precious promises: that by these ye might be partakers of the divine nature, having escaped the corruption that is in the world through lust.*
>
> *2 Peter 1:4*

As you F.I.G.H.T. for your marriage, it is important to choose the right weapons. Use weapons that are powerful enough to cast down the enemy's strongholds and strong enough to protect you from the enemy's fiery darts. "Above all, taking the shield of faith, wherewith ye shall be able to quench all the fiery darts of the wicked. And take the helmet of salvation, and the sword of the Spirit, which is the word of God" (Ephesians 6:16, 17). "For the word of God is quick, and powerful, and sharper than any two-edged sword, piercing even to the dividing asunder of soul and spirit, and of the joints and marrow, and is a discerner of the thoughts and intents of the heart" (Hebrews 4:12).

Soldier, when great power and strength are needed, the sword of the Spirit, God's Holy Word, and the shield of faith are excellent choices. When I was down, God's powerful Word lifted me. When I was hurt, His powerful Word healed me. When I was weak, God's strong arm helped me. Once I gained some strength, I was better equipped to lift my shield of faith and quench the enemy's darts of darkness, doubt and discouragement.

At the beginning of His earthly ministry, Jesus spent 40 days fasting and praying in the wilderness. When the fast was over, Jesus was hungry. Satan saw this as the perfect opportunity to tempt Jesus to sin and thwart the plan of salvation. Satan, the father of lies, spoke lies and tempted Jesus three times.

Jesus' response to each of Satan's temptations enables us to observe our great Leader as He skillfully uses the sword of the Spirit. Each time Jesus was tempted, He replied by speaking truth—for He is the way, the truth, and the life (John 14:6). He began his response with "It is written" and then proceeded with an applicable verse from the Old Testament scriptures (Matthew 4: 4, 7, 10). After three failed attempts, the Bible tells us Satan left Jesus, and angels came and ministered to Him (Matthew 4:11). Jesus successfully used the sword of the Spirit, and Satan was defeated. Jesus not only shows us how to properly use the sword, but He also shows us the results of its proper use—victory over Satan's temptations.

Soldiers in any army must spend time getting acquainted with their weapons. In time, they are expected to display a level of proficiency with their weapons to demonstrate they are prepared for active service. The same is true for soldiers in the Lord's army. Christian soldiers must spend time acquainting themselves with the sword of the Spirit, the truths of God's Word. Seek the truth; believe the truth; love the truth; rejoice in the truth; walk in the truth, and speak the truth. The more time we invest in studying the truths of the Bible, the better equipped we will be when the enemy comes to tempt us with darkness, doubt and discouragement.

When Satan tempts you with lies, should you listen? NO! Instead, follow Jesus' example and speak truth. "Sanctify them through thy truth: thy word is truth" (John 17:17). God's Word, the Holy Bible, is the truth we should speak. Spending time reading the truth will enable you to "know the truth, and the truth shall make you free" (John 8:32). You might ask, *"Free from what?" Free* from Satan's lies and errors, and *free* from being a slave to sin under his cruel tyranny.

Soldier, gird your loins with truth (Ephesians 6:14). Make it a habit to study the truths of God's Word daily and identify Bible promises. When there was a revival in my devotional life, I started reading a portion of Psalms each day. Before I read the Bible, I would pray and ask for the Holy Spirit to guide me and give me understanding. When a verse caught my attention, I would find related Bible texts by using a concordance or my Bible's marginal reference guide.

I was extremely brokenhearted when I started reading the book of Psalms, so I was delighted when I read Psalm 34:18, "The LORD is nigh unto them that are of a broken heart; and saveth such as be of a contrite spirit." As I read these words, I believed the Lord was speaking directly to me and reassuring me that He was close to me. His words brought me great comfort, and I wanted to hear more words like these from Him. Hence, I used my Bible's marginal reference guide and found Psalm 147:3, "He healeth the broken in heart, and bindeth up their wounds." *There was hope!* I thought to myself. *Jesus was promising to heal me and bind up my wounds!* I was thrilled to find these and many more treasures in the Bible that spoke to my aching heart. I clearly heard the voice of Jesus speaking to me through the pages of His written Word, and I was ready to give Him my undivided attention.

During my Bible study time, I continued to identify Bible promises that applied to my life. I wrote the Bible promises on index cards and referred to them several times throughout the day. When a verse was especially important to me, I posted it in various places around my home. As the days and weeks passed by, I realized I was doing something I had struggled to do most of my life—I was memorizing Bible verses. As my appreciation for the promises of the Bible increased, memorizing verses was no longer a difficult task, but a painless privilege.

> *Thy word have I hid in mine heart,*
> *that I might not sin against thee.*
> *Psalm 119:11*

When the enemy came to me with lies like, *"You are all alone, or you will be heartbroken forever,"* the Holy Spirit would mercifully bring Bible promises to my remembrance. Instead of choosing to believe Satan's lie, I chose instead to believe God's truth. *I was not all alone* because of God's promise in Psalm 34:18. *I would not be heartbroken forever* because of Psalm 147:3. When I chose to believe God's promises, the fiery darts of the enemy were quenched and lost their power in my life.

Over time, I had quite a collection of Bible promises pertaining to the love of God, comfort, hope, deliverance, healing, and other topics that were near to my heart during my separation from Brent. Eventually, I started identifying Bible promises for Brent and our marriage. When my Psalms study was over, I started reading the New Testament. The following was one of the first passages to catch my attention:

> *And Jesus went about all Galilee, teaching in their synagogues, and preaching the gospel of the kingdom, and healing all manner of sickness and all manner of disease among the people. And his fame went throughout all Syria: and they brought unto him all sick people that were taken with divers diseases and torments, and those which were possessed with devils, and those which were lunatic, and those that had the palsy;*
>
> *and he healed them.*
>
> *Matthew 4:23, 24*

I began to see Jesus' earthly ministry in a new way as I read the Gospels of Matthew, Mark, Luke, and John. The words "and he healed them" were like sweet music to my ears, because Brent needed healing; I needed healing, and our marriage needed healing. Since Jesus does not change (Malachi 3:6), and He was powerful enough to perform the numerous miracles recorded in the Gospels, I dared to believe He was powerful enough to work miracles to save my husband and our marriage.

When my studies took me to Mark 5 and Luke 8, my attention was especially drawn to the story of Jesus healing the demoniac in the country of the Gadarenes. The demoniac had a history of unusual behavior that included crying, cutting himself with stones, wearing no clothes, and living in the tombs. Jesus commanded the evil spirits to come out of the man, and they obeyed. Jesus spoke, and the man was healed. We find the man who was once known for living in the tombs and not wearing clothes, "sitting at the feet of Jesus, clothed, and in his right mind" (Luke 8:35).

I wanted Jesus to do the same thing for Brent. I wanted to find the man, who had once been known for leaving Jesus and his wife, sitting at the feet of Jesus and in his right mind. When I prayed, I often spoke words of faith and praised Jesus in advance for working a miracle in Brent's life and leading him to sit at His feet and be in his right mind. In His perfect timing, Jesus gave me the desires of my heart and brought these words to pass in Brent's life. I am so thankful to Jesus for what He did for my husband and our marriage.

As you identify and memorize Bible promises, the Holy Spirit can bring them to mind and help you quench the fiery darts of the enemy when he tries to discourage you and tempt you with his lies. You can also use Bible promises as a way to speak words of faith during your prayer time and praise the Lord for victory before it is even apparent. God gave us an example of speaking words of faith when He called Abraham "a father of many nations" before he had any children. He "calleth those things which be not as though they were" (Romans 4:17).

King Jehoshaphat and the people of Judah also chose to speak words of faith and praise when enemies came against them. The king stood before the people and encouraged them to believe in the Lord and in His prophets. Then, he assigned singers to go before the army praising the Lord and saying "Praise the LORD; for his mercy endureth for ever" (2 Chronicles 20:21). When they began to sing and to praise the Lord, He sent ambushments and defeated their enemies! Follow the example of Jehoshaphat—speak words of faith and praise the Lord for what He is doing and what He is going to do for you.

Make a commitment to become acquainted with your sword, the Word of God. Set aside time each day to prayerfully study your Bible and identify Bible promises. Claim these promises as you pray for your spouse, your marriage, and yourself.

Soldier, now that you have made a decision to fervently pray and identify Bible promises, it's time to *Give Thanks* to God!

REVIEW AND REFLECTION QUESTIONS

1. Which weapon is strong enough to protect you from the enemy's fiery darts? (Ephesians 6:16)

_____

_____

_____

2. What does it mean to have "your loins girt about with truth?" (Ephesians 6:14)

_____

_____

_____

3. How did Jesus respond each time He was tempted by Satan? (Matthew 4:4, 7, 10)

_____

_____

_____

4. How should we respond each time we are tempted by Satan?

_____

_____

_____

5. Summarize this chapter in one sentence.

_____

_____

_____

EXTRA STUDY

1. Read Luke 8:27-35. Describe the demoniac before and after he met Jesus.

_____

_____

_____

2. Read 2 Chronicles 20:1-22. Describe the events that occurred before Jehoshaphat and the people were delivered from their enemies.

_____

_____

_____

3. Read 2 Peter 1:4. When we are partakers of the divine nature, our lives will be guided by the true principles of God's Word, and we will humbly respond when the Holy Spirit brings conviction of sin. What has God given us to help us be partakers of the divine nature?

_____

_____

_____

TRY IT!

When Brent and I were separated, I identified Bible promises and claimed them as I prayed for Brent, our marriage, and myself. List a few of your own promises below. Try to memorize them!

_____

_____

_____

_____

_____

Bible Promises for You

* * *

Bible Promises to Consider When Praying for Your Spouse:

- » Proverbs 5:15-19
- » Jeremiah 24:7
- » Acts 3:19
- » Acts 26:18
- » 2 Timothy 2:25, 26
- » 2 Peter 3:9

Bible Promises to Consider When Praying for Your Marriage:

- » Psalm 90:15
- » Psalm 115:12
- » Joel 2:21, 25
- » Luke 1:37

Bible Promises to Consider When Praying for Yourself:

ENCOURAGEMENT

- » Job 42:10, 12
- » Psalm 34:18, 19
- » Psalm 147:3
- » Isaiah 61:3
- » 2 Corinthians 1:3, 4
- » 2 Corinthians 4:17, 18
- » Philippians 4:13
- » 2 Timothy 2:24-26
- » Hebrews 13:5

FORGIVENESS

- » Psalm 86:5
- » Matthew 6:14
- » Luke 6:37
- » 1 John 1:9

PATIENCE

- » Lamentations 3:25, 26
- » Galatians 6:9

WISDOM AND GUIDANCE

- » Psalm 32:8
- » Jeremiah 33:3

CHAPTER ELEVEN
GIVE THANKS

O give thanks unto the LORD, for he is good:
for his mercy endureth for ever.
Psalm 107:1

Once again we'll turn our attention to upright and courageous Paul. He was no stranger to hardships and affliction, yet he endured hardness like a good soldier for Jesus. Paul shares details pertaining to some of the trials he experienced as he faithfully served in the Lord's army:

Of the Jews five times received I forty stripes save one. Thrice was I beaten with rods, once was I stoned, thrice I suffered shipwreck, a night and a day I have been in the deep; In journeyings often, in perils of waters, in perils of robbers, in perils by mine own countrymen, in perils by the heathen, in perils in the city, in perils in the wilderness, in perils in the sea, in perils among false brethren; In weariness and painfulness, in watchings often, in hunger and thirst, in fastings often, in cold and nakedness. Beside those things that are without, that which cometh upon me daily,
the care of all the churches.
2 Corinthians 11:24-28

Despite all of these afflictions, under the inspiration of the Holy Spirit, Paul still writes, "In every thing give thanks: for this is the will of God in Christ Jesus concerning you" (1 Thessalonians 5:18). He not only admonished others to give thanks, but the Bible contains specific instances of Paul giving thanks for God's gift of Jesus, victory over sin, hope of eternal life, fellow believers, and for help he received from others. If Paul can give thanks, those of us who have experienced considerably fewer hardships can certainly give thanks.

"Know ye that the LORD he is God: it is he that hath made us, and not we ourselves; we are his people, and the sheep of his pasture. Enter into his gates with thanksgiving, and into his courts with praise: be thankful unto him, and bless his name" (Psalm 100:3, 4). God is our Creator. He takes care of us and blesses us every day. He is worthy of our thanksgiving and praise. Take time to acknowledge the blessings He gives you, and give thanks to Him every day.

Many professed Christians dwell too much on the dark side of life, when they might rejoice in the sunshine; they repine when they should be glad; they talk of trials when they should offer praise for the rich blessings they enjoy. They look at the unpleasant things, hoard up the disappointments, and sigh over the griefs, and, as a consequence, grow heavyhearted and sad, when, should they count up their blessings, they would find them so numerous that they would forget to mention their annoyances. If they would every day take note of the favors that are done them; if they would store their minds with the precious memory of kindnesses received, how much occasion they would find to render thanks and praise to the Giver of all good. [5]

A Thankful Journal is a tool that may help you remember to give thanks. I received my first journal as a gift when my family and I were serving in South Korea as missionaries in 2015. Due to language barriers between the thoughtful church member and myself, I didn't really understand the importance of or the "how-to" of using the journal. I recorded my blessings on an irregular basis, yet I continued to focus my attention on unpleasant things and disappointments on a regular basis. Like the "many professed Christians" mentioned in the quote above, I dwelt too much on the dark side of life. I thought I was keeping it "real," but I was only keeping it *real* negative.

Unfortunately, I missed out on a great opportunity to cultivate the habit of giving thanks. Instead of counting my blessings, I developed a bad habit of complaining and throwing myself pity parties. Looking back, I now realize that even in the midst of challenging living conditions, a small stipend, and trying to balance the demands of motherhood and missionary service I still had many reasons to give thanks. I should have been thankful we had a clean and safe place to live, money for groceries and other necessities, healthy children, and the opportunity to share Jesus with our Korean friends and neighbors.

Although there is still room for improvement, I've made significant progress since I received my first Thankful Journal. Last year, I started writing in my Thankful Journal on an almost daily basis, thus, cultivating the habit of *having an attitude of gratitude.* Instead of focusing on what's wrong, I am learning to focus on what's right and how good my Heavenly Father is. Taking time to reflect upon God's goodness towards me tends to have a positive, lasting influence upon my outlook for the rest of the day. It gives me fresh reminders that God has been good to me in the past, and regardless of the challenges I may face during the day, I can have confidence that His goodness will continue.

> . . . *Hitherto hath the LORD helped us.*
> *1 Samuel 7:12*
>
> *The LORD hath been mindful of us: he will bless us.*
> *Psalm 115:12*

Taking the time to write out what I was thankful for was a fairly easy, first step. The challenging part came when the time came to put it into practice. I struggled with practically applying the principle of thankfulness in my everyday life. For example, when Brent came home from work he often would ask me, "How was your day?" I would respond, "Fine" and then continue with a slew of bad news sprinkled with a little good news here and there. I was giving him an honest account of my day, but the tenure of my response was negative. As a result, I failed to make our home an attractive and welcoming place for Brent to return to after a long day at work.

Sadly and ironically, I failed to resist temptation and chose to murmur and complain about the trials that stemmed from being home with my children, the special gifts God blessed us with after He restored our marriage. Unfortunately, I listened to Satan's lies instead of counting my blessings and remembering that "children are an heritage of the Lord: and the fruit of the womb is his reward" (Psalm 127:3). Despite my negative responses, Brent continued to ask me about my day. From time to time he tried to gently express his concern about my negative outlook, but my eyes were blinded to the error of my ways. Instead of nagging me about my bad habit, my loving husband prayed for me. The Lord answered his prayer in an unexpected manner.

In 2017, I started participating in an online Christian parenting course. I joined the group in order to become a better parent, but the Lord had something greater in mind—He was answering Brent's prayers on my behalf. The Lord has used this group to help me become a better Christian, mother, *and* wife.

This year we are reading from a book called *Child Guidance,* and our facilitator often remarks that the title of the book may very well be *Parent Guidance,* because the Lord is teaching us so much as we read and discuss the book. The "aha moments" keep coming as we read and grasp the concept that we can't give our children what we don't have. In order to be effective Christian parents, we must look to Jesus for wisdom and help as we interact with our children, and then be willing to surrender to Him moment by moment. As we learn to love, trust, and obey Jesus, we can teach our children to do the same.

In His great mercy, the Lord used this parenting course to open my eyes and help me see the error of my ways. When I observed my children's attitudes and behaviors, I realized they were exhibiting the negative attitudes and behaviors I unintentionally modeled for them. I felt convicted that I needed a better attitude.

The Lord gently spoke to me and told me I needed to be what I wanted my children to be. How could I expect my children to rejoice in the Lord and give thanks in everything when I was struggling to do it? If I wanted my children to give thanks and have positive attitudes, then I needed to do the same, because my work as a parent includes providing faithful instruction from the Word of God *and* giving them a godly example.

I needed supernatural help to break this lifelong habit. Hence, I made this issue a matter of special prayer and started taking baby steps toward my goal. When Brent would ask me how my day was, I began putting on a smile and saying, "Great!" and shared as few details as possible about my day. After a couple of weeks, I realized my days *were* great—the Lord had been good to me, and I had many reasons to give thanks. Soon, Brent's inquiry about my day received a genuine, natural and unrehearsed "Great!," and I proceeded to tell him about all the great things the Lord did for me while he was away at work. When I shared news that wasn't the greatest, the Lord helped me state the facts without the usual "woe is me" attitude. Inwardly I rejoiced about my small victories, while outwardly Brent noticed a visible change in my attitude. It felt really good to hear him commend my efforts and express his appreciation to me for making our home a pleasant place.

In addition to helping you focus on what's right, entries in your Thankful Journal can also serve as a guide as you lift up your voice in praise and thanksgiving during your personal prayer time. Philippians 4:6 tells us to let our requests be made known unto God with thanksgiving. Christian soldier Daniel gives us an example of praying with thanksgiving after he heard of the king's decree to cast into the lion's den any person that prayed during a thirty-day period to any God or man besides the king (Daniel 6:7). The possibility of being thrown into a lion's den would have struck fear in the heart of the average person, but Daniel's faith in God prevailed. Instead of giving place to fear and compromise, Daniel remained calm and loyal to God and continued to kneel three times a day to pray and give thanks to God (Daniel 6:10).

"It is a good thing to give thanks unto the LORD, and to sing praises unto thy name, O most High" (Psalm 92:1). Follow the examples of Christian soldiers Paul and Daniel—in the midst of trouble and affliction, choose to give thanks.

Offer unto God thanksgiving . . .
Psalm 50:14

Soldier, now that you have made a decision to fervently pray, identify Bible promises, and give thanks, it's time to **Have Patience**!

REVIEW AND REFLECTION QUESTIONS

1. What should we give the Lord? (Psalm 107:1)

_____

_____

_____

2. Compare and contrast your life experiences with Paul's.
(2 Corinthians 11:24-28)

_____

_____

_____

3. What happens when we take the time to count our blessings?

_____

_____

_____

4. Do you tend to dwell on the dark side or rejoice in the sunshine? Explain.

_____

_____

_____

5. What did Daniel do after he heard the king's decree? (Daniel 6:10)

_____

_____

_____

6. List five things you are thankful for.

_____

_____

_____

7. Summarize this chapter in one sentence.

_____

_____

_____

EXTRA STUDY

A. Look up *thanks, thanksgiving or thankful* in a Bible concordance. Write the definition below.

_____

_____

_____

B. Choose one of your favorite verses and write it below. Try to memorize the verse this week.

_____

_____

_____

TRY IT!

Start keeping a Thankful Journal. You only need three things to get started right away—a notebook, an ink pen, and five minutes. Choose the time that works best for you, and establish a habit of writing in your journal at this time each day. Write the date at the top of each journal entry, and then list as many things as you can within your allotted time. At the end of each week, take time to review the blessings you recorded in your journal.

CHAPTER TWELVE
HAVE PATIENCE

> *The LORD is good unto them that wait for him, to the soul that seeketh*
> *him. It is good that a man should both hope and quietly*
> *wait for the salvation of the LORD.*
> *Lamentations 3:25, 26*

A s you fervently pray, identify Bible promises, and give thanks for your marriage, be sure to hope and quietly wait for the salvation of the Lord. Make a firm decision to have patience and keep looking to the Lord to save your spouse and your marriage. Consider the words of Jesus found in Mark 4:28, "For the earth bringeth forth fruit of herself; first the blade, then the ear, after that the full corn in the ear." At the right time, God's power and generous gifts of rain, air, and sunshine cause seeds to germinate. This same power can cause your marriage to be restored—so have patience.

Luke 8:15 tells us, "The seed is the word of God." Let us sow the good seed in our hearts by believing, prayerfully studying, memorizing, and practically applying God's Word. If we bountifully sow God's Word in our hearts, we shall bountifully reap (2 Corinthians 9:6). God promises that His Word shall not return unto

Him void, but it will accomplish what He pleases and prosper where He sends it (Isaiah 55:11). As we patiently do our part sowing God's Word in our hearts, God will do His part and cause His Word to go forth and produce results in our lives and in our marriages.

Let's learn some practical lessons from seed sowing. My family and I enjoy the taste of freshly picked, home grown produce, so we started a small garden a few years ago. We often start our seeds on a table in our family room near a couple of large windows. Even though the seeds are in the soil and hidden from our sight, we continue to water them because things are happening beneath the soil that we can't see. As the days, weeks, and months pass, we must patiently wait for the plants to germinate, grow, and ripen. At the appointed time our patience pays off, and we are rewarded with luscious, flavorful produce that surpasses what's typically found in your average grocery store.

Can your husband's heart be compared to soil with a "seed" buried beneath the surface? Yes! It may look like nothing is happening, but you don't know how the Holy Spirit is moving upon the soil of your husband's heart, so you must have patience. Step out in faith and plant abundant seeds of love and kindness in your husband's life. "In the morning sow thy seed, and in the evening withold not thine hand: for thou knowest not whether shall prosper, either this or that, or whether they both shall be alike good" (Ecclesiastes 11:6). As you patiently endure challenging circumstances, believe God's promise that, "they that sow in tears shall reap in joy" (Psalm 126:5).

Let's learn another lesson from seeds. Seeds have needs. In order to ensure proper development, we try to provide the right soil, the right temperature, and sufficient water for our seeds. If the needs of the seeds are met, we can expect to see sprouts in about a week.

After six to eight weeks, we *should* have seedlings that are ready to be transplanted. I say 'should,' because sometimes our plants don't make it past the seedling stage.

There are several reasons seedlings fail to thrive, but in our home the top three reasons are too little water, too much water, or too much handling by curious little boys. Unfortunately, there are times when my sons get tired of waiting, and they pluck the tender seedling out of the soil. Their impatience causes them to lose some of the rewards that await the patient gardener at harvest time.

Can these gardening lessons apply to your marriage? Yes! Have you ever been tempted to "give too little water" by failing to share kind words or deeds with your husband? Have you ever been tempted to "drown the tender seedling" with a flood of angry, impatient words? Have you ever been tempted to "pluck the tender seedling," give up on your marriage and forfeit the possibility of reaping a happy marriage? Don't pluck the tender seedling! Instead, tenderly nourish the seedling and patiently wait for the Lord to bring healing to your relationship with your spouse. Don't be weary in well doing, for in due season you shall reap, if you faint not (Galatians 6:9).

When Brent moved out in 2000, I thought he would change his mind rather quickly and return home within a couple of months. This did not happen. As a matter of fact, he didn't even return home within a couple of years. It took four years of F.I.G.H.T.ing before I saw any evidence of God working in Brent's life! I sowed in tears and had patience, and now I am reaping in joy as Brent's wife and mother of Madison, Samuel, Daniel, Anthony-Joseph, and Michael-Shepherd.

Brent's favorite Bible verse says, "But he that shall endure unto the end, the same shall be saved" (Matthew 24:13). Endure hardness like a good soldier for Jesus, and have patience as you look to Him to save your marriage. If you fail to endure hardness and F.I.G.H.T. for your marriage, the likelihood of it being saved is greatly diminished. Therefore, make a commitment to keep praying for your marriage no matter how long it takes. If you fail to see results in a week, a month, or even a year—have patience and keep praying. Harvest times vary, so, no matter how long it takes, have patience and keep praying— *your marriage is worth it!*

Job, a faithful soldier in the Lord's army, gives us an excellent example of patience. He patiently endured hardness and is described as "perfect and upright, and one that feared God and eschewed evil" (Job 1:1). Satan requested and received permission from God to test Job's loyalty to Him. Satan wanted to see if Job would remain faithful if his blessings were taken away, so during the testing period, Job lost his children, his livestock, and many of his servants. How did Job respond? "Then Job arose, and rent his mantle, and shaved his head, and fell down upon the ground, and worshipped, And said, Naked came I out of my mother's womb, and naked shall I return thither: the LORD gave, and the LORD hath taken away; blessed be the name of the LORD" (Job 1:20, 21). Job praised God, trusted Him, and remained loyal to Him. What a powerful example for us to follow!

Later, Satan smote Job "with sore boils from the sole of his foot unto his crown" (Job 2:7). Job continued to remain loyal to God. In the midst of his test, Job continued to speak words of faith. "But he knoweth the way that I take: when he hath tried me, I shall come forth as gold" (Job 23:10). Job's words came to pass, and he came forth from the test purified and refined.

Job patiently endured, and he was rewarded. "And the LORD

turned the captivity of Job, when he prayed for his friends: also the LORD gave Job twice as much as he had before. So the LORD blessed the latter end of Job more than his beginning: for he had fourteen thousand sheep, and six thousand camels, and a thousand yoke of oxen, and a thousand she asses. He had also seven sons and three daughters." (Job 42:10, 12, 13). Are you ready for the Lord to turn your captivity, bless you, and give you more than you had before?

> *Behold, we count them happy which endure. Ye have heard of the patience of Job, and have seen the end of the Lord; that the Lord is very pitiful, and of tender mercy.*
> *James 5:11*

Hope and quietly wait for the salvation of the Lord, soldier. He is working all things out for your good. His timing is not our timing. His timing is much better than ours. The Lord is ready, willing, and able to give you "beauty for ashes, the oil of joy for mourning, the garment of praise for the spirit of heaviness"(Isaiah 61:3), but you must fervently pray, identify Bible promises, give thanks, and have patience. Now, let's *Take Time for Testimonies*!

REVIEW AND REFLECTION QUESTIONS

1. What should we hope and quietly wait for? (Lamentations 3:26)

_____

_____

_____

2. What are two practical lessons we can learn from seeds?

_____

_____

_____

3. Compare and contrast your life experiences with Job's.

_____

_____

_____

4. When did the Lord turn Job's captivity? (Job 42:10)

_____

_____

_____

5. What did the Lord give Job in the end? (Job 42:12, 13)

_____

_____

_____

6. Summarize this chapter in one sentence.

_____

_____

_____

EXTRA STUDY

Read the following Bible verses about patience. How can you apply
each verse to your marriage?

Psalm 27:14

_____

_____

Romans 5:3-5

_____

_____

Romans 12:12

_____

_____

Hebrews 12:1-3

_____

_____

2 Peter 1:4-7

_____

_____

James 1:3, 4

_____

_____

TRY IT!

A. Read the quote below.

> *The Lord turned the captivity of Job when he prayed, not only for himself, but for those who were opposing him. When he felt earnestly desirous that the souls that had trespassed against him might be helped, he himself received help. Let us pray, not only for ourselves, but for those who have hurt us, and are continuing to hurt us. Pray, pray, especially in your mind. Give not the Lord rest; for His ears are open to hear sincere, importunate prayers, when the soul is humbled before Him.* [6]

B. Who are your opposers? Take time to pray for them daily.

_____

_____

_____

CHAPTER THIRTEEN
TAKE TIME FOR TESTIMONIES

> *And they overcame him by the blood of the Lamb, and by the word of their testimony; and they loved not their lives unto the death.*
> *Revelation 12:11*

tanding before a large crowd gathered on the day of Pentecost, Peter testified about Jesus' life, death, and resurrection. Afterwards, three thousand souls gladly received his testimony and were baptized (Acts 2:41)! Peter took time for testimonies, and thousands were baptized.

Does God want to use you to win souls for His Kingdom, like He used Peter? Yes, He does! In the armory of a Christian soldier, testimonies can be used to break down the enemy's strongholds that enshroud souls with darkness and doubt. Only God knows the far-reaching impact a testimony can have upon souls in darkness who are searching for the light found only in His Word.

The testimonies of Sheila and the other leaders of the support group greatly encouraged me to F.I.G.H.T. for my marriage. The women shared honest and transparent testimonies, yet the Lord seasoned their words with grace that covered the sins of their spouses and preserved the dignity of the sacred family circle. Many tears were shed in Sheila's living room, but we rejoiced when broken marriages were restored like the marriage in the following testimony:

A close family friend, Paula,[7] often joined me at Sheila's house for prayer, worship, and praise. She was married to her high-school sweetheart, Scott,[8] and to this union four children were born. Scott, a veteran with over 26 years of military service, served in Vietnam and Operation Desert Storm. As a result of his service, he suffered from many visible and invisible wounds, including Post Traumatic Stress Disorder (PTSD), which eventually led to self-medication with drugs. Scott's poor choices caused much suffering for him, his wife, his marriage, and his family.

Despite the challenges, Scott's family trusted in God, prayed for, supported, and helped him get treatment. The Lord showed Himself strong on behalf of this family. In due time, Scott rededicated his life to Christ, and his broken relationships with family members were restored. After eleven months of separation, Scott and Paula were remarried in front of family, friends, and other well-wishers. Now, they are enjoying their retirement years with their children and grandchildren. To God be the glory for great things He has done!

Jesus wants you to be both a minister and a witness to lift up the wounded and turn them from darkness to light and from doubt to belief. Diligently watch for opportunities to share your testimony and "speak a word in season to him that is weary" (Isaiah 50:4). The Lord promises to be with your mouth and teach you what you should say (Exodus 4:12).

Sheila shared her testimony with the ladies in her home. I shared my testimony with you. So when the Lord restores your marriage, be sure to share your testimony with others. However, you don't have to wait until you have a marriage testimony. You can start now.

The Holy Spirit can use your personal conversion testimony to bring conviction to the hearts of sinners and help them choose Jesus and eternal life instead of Satan and death. Seeing the difference Jesus made in your life may inspire others with hope that the gospel of Christ has power to change lives and save souls!

> *For we ourselves also were sometimes foolish, disobedient, deceived, serving divers lusts and pleasures, living in malice and envy, hateful, and hating one another. But after that the kindness and love of God our Saviour toward man appeared, Not by works of righteousness which we have done, but according to his mercy he saved us, by the washing of regeneration, and renewing of the Holy Ghost; Which he shed on us abundantly through Jesus Christ our Saviour; That being justified by his grace, we should be made heirs according to the hope of eternal life.*
>
> *Titus 3:3-7*

As you encounter individuals with heavy hearts and heavy burdens, you can encourage them to endure the hard times and look forward to a time in heaven when "God shall wipe away all tears from their eyes; and there shall be no more death, neither sorrow, nor crying, neither shall there be any more pain" (Revelation 21:4). On other occasions, you may see fit to share personal testimonies pertaining to how the Lord has helped you, led you, provided for you, and protected you. Your testimony may help someone in the valley of decision choose marriage over divorce or life over suicide. Therefore, pray for the Holy Ghost and for boldness as you share your testimonies on the Master's behalf.

The Lord has helped countless soldiers "make known his deeds among the people" (Psalm 105:1), and He will help you, too. You may not be called to share your testimony before a group as large as the one Peter stood before, but the Lord still wants you to tell others what He has done for you. You can start by sharing entries from your Thankful Journal with your family or friends.

My family and I share testimonies with each other on a daily basis, but each Friday evening we gather for a special worship to acknowledge the seventh-day Sabbath (Exodus 20:8-11) and express our gratitude for the blessings God bestowed upon us during the week. This is one of the highlights of our week—a refreshing time of reflection that draws us closer to each other and to our Creator. After praying and singing, we take turns sharing what we are thankful for. Two-year-old Michael-Shepherd even chimes in with his simple words of praise and thanksgiving.

Once you are comfortable sharing your testimonies with your family, venture out from home-base and expand your territory. Take time to share your testimonies with your church family, neighbors, friends, co-workers, and others you may come in contact with. Our family has often been strengthened and encouraged by the testimonies given by fellow believers during midweek prayer meetings. In addition to listening to the testimonies of others, we have been privileged to share what God has done for us.

Testimonies are a good way for believers to strengthen and encourage one another in their Christian experience. They are also an effective means of sharing Jesus and the Gospel with unbelievers. Add *Take Time for Testimonies* to your armory, and report to duty *immediately*. Consider yourself fully equipped with indispensable, unfailing weapons from God's Word to help you accomplish your mission, Soldier!

Remember, our God is a God of reconciliation, and He has given us the ministry of reconciliation (2 Corinthians 5:18). May He bless your efforts towards reconciliation with your spouse and bring complete healing to your marriage. Your broken marriage is worth every tear, every prayer, and every moment of time you invest to restore it. Now go forward in faith, and F.I.G.H.T. for your marriage!

>> **F**ervently Pray.

>> **I**dentify Bible Promises.

>> **G**ive Thanks.

>> **H**ave Patience.

>> **T**ake Time for Testimonies.

REVIEW AND REFLECTION QUESTIONS

1. How do the individuals mentioned in Revelation 12:11 overcome?

_____

_____

_____

2. What promise does the Lord make to us in Exodus 4:12?

_____

_____

_____

3. Write a one sentence summary about Titus 3:3-7.

_____

_____

_____

4. How has the Lord helped, led, provided for, or protected you this week?

_____

_____

_____

5. Have you shared any testimonies this week? If so, keep sharing. If not, start sharing.

_____

_____

_____

6. Summarize this chapter in one sentence.

_____

_____

_____

EXTRA STUDY

Paul's imprisonment gave him the opportunity to take the Gospel to kings, princes and rulers. Read Paul's conversion testimony in Acts 26. Use Paul's testimony and the outline below to help you write your own personal conversion testimony. Be ready and willing to share your testimony, when the opportunity arises to do so.

A. Description of Your Old Life Before Jesus

_____

_____

_____

B. Description of Your New Life with Jesus

_____

_____

_____

C. Invitation for Listener(s) to Accept Jesus as Lord and Savior

_____

_____

_____

TRY IT!

Talk to your family about coming together for a time of prayer and testimonies each Friday evening. Begin the service with a word of prayer thanking the Lord for bringing your family and you safely through another week. Give each family member the opportunity to share his or her testimonies. Encourage everyone to share something—even if it is only one thing.

The following prompts may be helpful with younger children:

What happened this week that made you happy?

What happened this week that made you smile?

What's something special Jesus did for you this week?

OFFICIAL ORDERS

Now it's time for you to go forward and accomplish your mission. Your official orders are as follows:

1. Complete all Review and Reflection questions, Extra Study questions, and Try It exercises.

2. Remember the real enemy is Satan, not your spouse.

3. Put on the whole armor of God.

4. Incorporate the G.E.T. R.E.A.D.Y. health principles in your life daily.

5. Fervently pray for your spouse, your marriage, and yourself daily.

6. Identify and claim Bible promises for your spouse, your marriage, and yourself daily.

7. Give thanks to God daily.

8. Have patience as you wait for your prayers to be answered.

9. Take time for testimonies.

10. Go forward in faith, and with God's help *F.I.G.H.T. for Your Marriage*!

> *I have fought a good fight, I have finished my course, I have kept the faith.*
> *2 Timothy 4:7*

Sound the battle cry! See, the foe is nigh;
Raise the standard high for the Lord;
Gird your armor on, stand firm every one:
Rest your cause upon His holy Word.

Strong to meet the foe, marching on we go,
While our cause we know, must prevail;
Shield and banner bright,
gleaming in the light,
Battling for the right we ne'er can fail.

O! Thou God of all, hear us when we call,
Help us one and all by Thy grace;
When the battle's done,
and the vict'ry's won,
May we wear the crown before Thy face.

Refrain: Rouse, then, soldiers,
rally round the banner,
Ready, steady, pass the word along;
Onward, forward, shout aloud, "Hosanna!"
Christ is Captain of the mighty throng.

~ William F. Sherwin ~

APPENDIX

GET READY

- » Get fresh air daily.
- » Exercise regularly.
- » Trust in God.
- » Retire for the night by 10:00 PM.
- » Eat healthy foods.
- » Aim to get 15 minutes of sunlight daily.
- » Drink lots of water.
- » Yield not to drugs and alcohol.

Get fresh air daily.

We can live weeks without food, days without water, but only minutes without oxygen. Every cell of the body requires a constant supply of oxygen brought to it by the blood. Air is a mixture of about 78% nitrogen, 21% oxygen and very small amounts of argon and carbon dioxide. According to authors Rico Hill and Jared Thurmon, "The more oxygen the body receives, the healthier the cells of the body will be. The healthier the cells are, the better your overall health."[9]

When an insufficient supply of oxygen is received, "the blood moves sluggishly . . . the brain is clouded; the thoughts are confused; gloom settles upon the spirits; the whole system becomes depressed and inactive, and peculiarly susceptible to disease."[10] Deep breathing is a great way to increase oxygen levels. Before breakfast, go outside for a few minutes to thank God for a new day, observe things in nature, and breathe deeply. This can be repeated throughout the day especially when you feel down or sluggish.

APPLY IT!

1. Keep your bedroom windows cracked so fresh air can circulate.
2. Avoid inhaling chemicals and toxins by staying away from cigarette smoke and switching to non-toxic personal care and household products.

Exercise regularly.

Inactivity weakens the system, but exercise strengthens the systems of the body. According to an article by the Center for Disease Control or CDC, "Regular physical activity is one of the most important things you can do for your health."[11] Another CDC article states exercise can keep your thinking, learning, and judgment skills sharp; reduce your risk of depression; lower the risk of many cancers; and reduce your risk of dying early from leading causes of death such as heart disease and diabetes.[12]

If you are new to exercising, walking is a simple way to get started. Schedule a daily walk with realistic goals based upon a certain number of steps, a specific distance, or a specific amount of time. Start slowly, and work your way up to a brisk walk of 3,000 steps, 1.5 miles, or 30 minutes a day three to five times a week.

APPLY IT!

1. Make daily exercise a priority in your life.
2. Set realistic goals, and use a pedometer, watch, or app to help you track your progress.

NOTE: Please consult with your medical provider before beginning or changing your exercise routine.

Trust in God.

> *Trust in the LORD with all thine heart;*
> *and lean not unto thine own understanding.*
> *Proverbs 3:5*

At the beginning of 2018, I was facing some extremely stressful situations, and I had difficulty coping. I felt pretty discouraged and low from time to time, but my Heavenly Father and my husband were the only ones who were aware of my struggles. I didn't mention it to anyone else because I didn't think anyone else could understand. After a few months, I finally decided to reach out to Leuanna, a friend of mine who also has five children. I thought about calling her in the past, but I hesitated because I figured she would be too busy to help. Much to my surprise, Leuanna and I were able to talk. Our phone conversation was brief, but her advice made a huge impact upon my life.

After a word of prayer, Leuanna quietly listened to what I had to say. Then, she cut right to the heart of the matter and reminded me of the importance of focusing my thoughts on the truths of God's Word. Finally, she challenged me to start writing in my Thankful

Journal every evening before bed. Like Naaman who doubted whether dipping in the river seven times would cure him of leprosy, I had my doubts as to whether or not Leuanna's simple suggestion could make a difference in my life. Nevertheless, I decided to heed the counsel of my dear friend, and I started writing in my Thankful Journal on a daily basis.

The Lord blessed, and I found Leuanna's suggestion to be a highly effective solution for my gloomy state of mind. I stopped focusing on what was wrong in my life, and I started focusing on what was right and the goodness of my Heavenly Father. As I reflected upon God's past blessings, my trust in Him increased, and I gained confidence that He who helped me in the past would help me today and in the future.

According to Celeste Lee, "Worry, anxiety, discontent, depression, [and] gloominess all have a negative influence on the body. These kinds of emotions tend to break down our life forces by inhibiting the systems of the body to function properly and actually invite decay, disease, and death."[13] On the other hand, Lee believes that trust in God promotes circulation, helps in the digestion process, gives energy to the nerves and soothes them, and strengthens the immune system.[14] This is not hard to believe because the Bible tells us in Proverbs 17:22 that "A merry heart doeth good like a medicine: but a broken spirit drieth the bones." This verse makes it clear that there is a link between our mental and our physical health.

APPLY IT!

1. Choose to stress less, and trust God more.
2. Cultivate an attitude of gratitude.

Retire for the night by 10:00 PM.

Due to modern conveniences, the average Westerner struggles to get seven hours of sleep at night. Time that should be devoted to rest is often spent working, reading, watching television, using electronic devices, etc. When we miss out on rest, we miss out on rest's benefits—vigor of body and mind. Rest has a positive effect on the cells of the immune system, aids the learning process, and promotes the repairing of our bodies. On the other hand, according to Vance Ferrell, "The go, go attitude so common to Western civilization, leads many to nervous breakdowns."[15]

Can a lack of rest have a negative impact upon your marriage? Consider the following experience of Beth,[16] a friend of mine who was having marital problems. After reading an early draft of this book that did not contain the eight health principles, she was hopeful that her marriage could be restored. However, weeks passed and things were still rocky between Beth and her husband, Frank[17.] Beth and I continued to pray for her marriage even though there was very little outward evidence of any improvements.

Several weeks later, Beth called me with some exciting news—her marriage was revitalized! After much prayer and fasting, the Lord revealed to her they were not getting enough sleep. Once Beth and Frank started getting in bed earlier, their relationship started improving. They began to enjoy each other's company like a pair of newlyweds! A lack of rest is probably not the only thing stopping you and your spouse from enjoying a happy marriage, but it is worth considering.

If you find yourself having trouble falling asleep, take a look at the following tips from neuroscientist and sleep researcher, Matthew Walker:

1. Keep a consistent sleep schedule. Go to bed and wake up at the same times daily.
2. Keep your bedroom dark and cool at night.
3. Refrain from using your bed as a place where you work, read, use electronic devices, or watch television. Train your brain to associate getting in bed with going to sleep.
4. Avoid caffeine and alcohol. These substances can still be found in the body several hours after consumption, and they make it difficult to get a good night's sleep.[18]

APPLY IT!

1. Set a goal to get in bed by 10:00 PM nightly.
2. Start winding down and lower the lighting in your home a couple of hours before bedtime.
3. Make plans to eat your last meal several hours before bedtime, so your stomach and entire digestive tract will be able to rest with the other organs of your body.

Eat healthy foods.

As a soldier in God's army, we want healthy bodies and clear minds that are ready to receive and carry out orders. Therefore it is imperative that we make wise food choices. In order to gain or maintain the best state of health, we need to eat the right amounts of the right foods at the right time. Choose a well-balanced diet consisting of a variety of fresh fruits, fresh vegetables, whole grains, legumes, nuts, and seeds. Keep your meals healthy, appetizing, and simple. Avoid heavily spiced foods, because they tend to irritate the stomach and cause cravings for stronger stimulants like drugs and alcohol.[19]

Daniel and his friends chose a simple diet and said no to the king's food and alcohol (Daniel 1:8). They were able to stand up for God and His truth even in the face of death (Daniel 3 and 6). The Bible also tells us of Jesus' simple diet. Isaiah 7:14, 15 says, "Therefore the Lord himself shall give you a sign; Behold, a virgin shall conceive, and bear a son, and shall call his name Immanuel. Butter and honey shall he eat, that he may know to refuse the evil, and choose the good." Jesus' unbroken communion with His Heavenly Father was the most important contributing factor to His successful resistance of all Satan's temptations, but based upon these verses, His simple diet was also a key factor.

APPLY IT!

1. Eat a variety of fresh fruits, fresh vegetables, whole grains, legumes, nuts, and seeds on a daily basis.
2. Plan to have your meals at regular times, at least five hours apart. The stomach functions best on a regular schedule.

Aim to get 15 minutes of sunlight daily.

Spending time in the sun has several benefits. According to Rico Hill and Jared Thurmon, sunlight is an effective immune system stimulant and an antibacterial, antifungal, and antiviral agent. Sunlight also naturally relieves stress and lowers blood pressure and cholesterol.[20]

Unfortunately, many of us miss out on the benefits of sunlight because we spend so much of our work, recreational, and rest time indoors. At the same time, modern conveniences like online shopping with in-home delivery, grocery pick-up, and drive-thru windows make it even easier for us to stay in our homes and vehicles instead of being out in the sunlight. As a result, we must be intentional about getting sunlight daily. Aim to spend 15 minutes in the sun, reflecting upon the goodness of the Son.

APPLY IT!

1. Go outside and expose your face and hands to sunlight for 15 minutes a day.
2. Open your curtains and blinds so the sunshine can come in.

Drink lots of water.

In health and in sickness, pure water is one of heaven's choicest blessings. Its proper use promotes health. It is the beverage which God provided to quench the thirst of animals and man. Drunk freely, it helps to supply the necessities of the system and assists nature to resist disease.[21]

Our bodies need water in order to function properly. When we don't get the water we need, we can experience mental confusion, lack of clarity, depression, impatience, the formation of gall stones, calcification in the joints (arthritic pain), mental fatigue, irritability, and slower metabolism (leading to weight gain).[22] On the other hand, there are numerous benefits associated with drinking lots of water. Water helps with digestion, proper organ function, and toxin and waste removal. Water also carries nutrients to cells, cushions your joints, and lowers high blood pressure and high blood sugar.[23]

Whether it's working, eating, or spending time with family and friends, people often schedule time for what's important for them. With this in mind, consider creating a water consumption schedule to make your daily water goals more attainable. For example, if your goal is to drink 8 glasses of water per day, plan to drink four glasses of water before lunch and four glasses of water after lunch. Plan to drink water first thing in the morning as you commune with Jesus, the Fountain of Living Waters, after each bathroom break, as you transition between activities, before and after exercising, and at other predetermined times during the day. Since drinking water with meals tends to interfere with digestion, plan to drink water between your meals.

Use the following formula to determine
your personal daily water needs:

Body weight (lbs.) ÷ 16 = number of 8 oz glasses/day

FOR EXAMPLE:

150 (weight in lbs.) ÷ 16 = 9.38 glasses/day

Thus, a person who weighs 150 lbs.

should drink a minimum of 9 ½ glasses of water daily.

APPLY IT!

1. Carry a reusable water bottle with you as a reminder to drink water throughout the day.
2. Establish water-drinking goals and routines.

Yield not to drugs and alcohol.

Unfortunately, most of us know someone whose drug or alcohol abuse has caused them to lose their job, home, family, or sanity. The use of drugs and alcohol can cause a once rational being to become irrational. Such was the case with Nadab and Abihu. These men were Moses' nephews and priests in the earthly tabernacle. Their sad story is recorded for us in Leviticus 10. These men were entrusted with great responsibility, but they failed to follow God's explicit orders pertaining to the services of the tabernacle. They lost their lives as a result of their poor choices and irreverent misconduct. After their death, the Lord proclaimed the following words to their father, Aaron, "Do not drink wine nor strong drink" (Leviticus 10:9).

Nadab and Abihu made unwise choices that negatively impacted God's tabernacle or dwelling place. Our bodies are also God's dwelling place (1 Corinthians 3:16), so we want to make wise choices that positively impact our bodies. As soldiers in the Lord's army, we don't want to do anything that destroys our health or impairs our thinking and ability to receive and implement orders from Jesus. As a result, it would be wise for us to conform not to the world's standards, but to do a reasonable service and present our bodies a living sacrifice, holy, acceptable unto God (Romans 12:1, 2). In order to do this, we must stay away from drugs, alcohol, and other health destroying substances and activities.

APPLY IT!

1. Educate yourself about the dangers of drug and alcohol use.
2. Refuse to use drugs and alcohol.

Notes

[1]White, E. *Education*. Mountain View, CA: Pacific Press Publishing Association, 1952. 257,258.

[2]White, E. *Patriarchs and Prophets*. Washington, D.C.: Review and Herald Publishing Association, 1958. 146, 147.

[3]White, E. *The Adventist Home*. Hagerstown, MD: Review and Herald Publishing Association, 1952. 270.

[4]White, E. *Ministry of Healing*. Mountain View, CA: Pacific Press Publishing Association, 1942. 143.

[5]White, E. *My Life Today*. Washington, D.C.: Review and Herald Publishing Association, 1952. 327.

[6]White, E. *Letter 88*. March 9, 1906.

[7]This is a pseudonym used to protect the privacy of the individual.

[8]This is a pseudonym used to protect the privacy of the individual.

[9]Hill, R. & Thurmon, J. *Healthy Self*. Berrien Springs, MI: Pan de Vida Publishers, 2017. 162.

[10]White, E. *Ministry of Healing*. Mountain View, CA: Pacific Press Publishing Association, 1942. 273.

[11]Centers for Disease Control and Prevention. (2009). https://www.cdc.gov/healthyplaces/healthtopics/physactivity.htm

[12]Centers for Disease Control and Prevention. (2018). https://www.cdc.gov/features/physical-activity/index.html

[13]Lee, C. *Understanding the Body Organs and the Eight Laws of Health.* Fort Oglethorpe, GA: Teach Services, Inc., 2004. 71.

[14]Ibid. 73.

[15]Ferrell, V. & Cherne, H. *Natural Remedies Encyclopedia.* Beersheba Springs, TN: Harvestime Books, 2008. 48.

[16]This is a pseudonym used to protect the privacy of the individual.

[17]This is a pseudonym used to protect the privacy of the individual.

[18]Anwar, Y. (2017). *Everything You Need to Know About Sleep, but Are Too Tired to Ask.* https://news.berkeley.edu/2017/10/17/whywesleep/.

[19]White, E. *Counsels on Diet and Foods.* Washington, D.C.: Review and Herald Publishing Association, 1976. 235.

[20]Hill, R. & Thurmon, J. *Healthy Self.* Berrien Springs, MI: Pan de Vida Publishers, 2017. 68.

[21]White, E. *Ministry of Healing.* Mountain View, CA: Pacific Press Publishing Association, 1942. 237.

[22]Hill, R. & Thurmon, J. *Healthy Self.* Berrien Springs, MI: Pan de Vida Publishers, 2017. 115.

[23]Ibid. 114.

QUESTIONS AND ANSWERS WITH ANIKA

Q: Were you ever afraid that Brent would leave you again?

A: That's a great question! Yes, I realized there was the possibility that Brent could leave again just like washed pigs return to the mud (2 Peter 2:22). However, I can't say that was ever a big concern of mine. Instead, I dared to believe in God's power to change lives and provide complete, lasting healing to our marriage. I believed the demoniac stayed clothed, in his right mind, and in a loving relationship with Jesus. I also believed the blind received their sight and maintained their sight.

At the same time, I witnessed the Lord do some incredible, miraculous things in my life and in Brent's life. Hence, my trust in God was strong enough to believe that He which hath begun a good work in Brent would perform it until the day of Jesus Christ. Therefore, I was confident in Brent's complete and lasting deliverance from the chains of the enemy (Philippians 1:6).

Finally, Isaiah 66:9 says, "Shall I bring to the birth, and not cause to bring forth? saith the LORD: shall I cause to bring forth, and shut the womb? saith thy God." I chose to apply these principles to Brent and to our marriage. I didn't believe the Lord brought us this far only to leave us. In my opinion, a failed second marriage for Brent and me would be similar to the Lord bringing forth and then "shutting the womb."

Q: How were you able to trust Brent again?

A: That's another great question! My trust in Brent didn't return over night. It took many years for Brent to regain my trust. It has been and still is a process. The second time around, our first year

139

of marriage was pretty rocky. We were trying to reestablish our home and adjust to our new roles as husband and wife and father and mother. We had to invest time building our foundation on the Rock, Jesus Christ, and put proper boundaries in place to protect our marriage.

We loved each other and were committed to making our marriage work, but love didn't wipe away the painful memories of the past. Brent understood the pain his poor choices caused me, so he was sincere and intentional about regaining my trust. At the same time, he was very patient with me and didn't try to force or rush me to trust him. Eventually, the hurts of the past were healed and replaced with trust and confidence.

Q: Did you ever doubt Brent's love for you once you were back together?

A: Yes, I did. In the beginning of our second marriage, I was still fairly inexperienced as a wife and had a lot to learn. When Brent didn't do what I wanted him to do, I questioned his love for me. For example, Brent enjoys spending time in nature and taking prayer walks. He would slip away for quiet time in the wooded area behind our house and leave me to get breakfast ready with an infant that wanted to be held and a hungry toddler. He seemed to be oblivious to things that needed attention around the house like meal preparation, dirty dishes, and little children. I thought these were obvious needs, and I wondered how he could really love me, if he wouldn't help me.

Both of us had a lot of learning and unlearning to do. Today, instead of doubting Brent's love, I try to communicate with him and ask for help instead of getting upset with him for not reading my mind. Today, Brent's eyes are open to the needs of our household, and he checks with me to see if I need any help before he heads off to his favorite places in nature. By God's grace, he is a loving, attentive husband and an actively involved father.

Thank You

Thank you for reading my book! If you enjoyed *FIGHT for Your Marriage* or found it helpful, I'd be very grateful if you'd tell others about it and post a short review on Amazon. Your support really does make a difference. I read the reviews personally, so I can get your feedback and make improvements.

Thanks again for your support!

-Anika

Note from the Author

Although I am an advocate of reconciliation, I recognize this may not be the best choice in cases where domestic violence is involved. If this is your case, please seek godly counsel and put proper boundaries in place. Address issues of personal safety and the safety of your children before you seek to be reconciled with your spouse.

Visit fightforyourmarriagetoday.com!

Be sure to join our email subscriber list so you can receive important updates about new products, special events, and special offers.

FIGHT for Your Marriage Journal

Give Thanks is one of the indispensable weapons you can use as you FIGHT for your marriage. Record your blessings in our attractive *FIGHT for Your Marriage Journal*. In addition to providing you with plenty of space to write, this journal includes many of the powerful Bible verses mentioned in *FIGHT for Your Marriage*. Get your *FIGHT for Your Marriage Journal* today!

FIGHT for Your Marriage
Support Group Leader's Guide

Are you interested in starting a support group similar to the one Sheila held in her home? If so, this book is for you! It contains valuable information that will help you minister to others and lead out with a *FIGHT for Your Marriage* support group.

Made in the
USA
Columbia, SC